Enduring CSS

Learn to really THINK about CSS, and how to create CSS
that endures continual iteration, multiple authors, and yet
always produces predictable results

Ben Frain

BIRMINGHAM - MUMBAI

Enduring CSS

First published: January 2017

Production reference: 2120117

Published by Packt Publishing Ltd.
Livery Place
35 Livery Street
Birmingham
B3 2PB, UK.
ISBN 978-1-78728-280-3

www.packtpub.com

Credits

Author

Ben Frain

Acquisition Editor

Dominic Shakeshaft

Technical Editor

Devesh Chugh

Indexer

Pratik Shirodkar

Production Coordinator

Deepika Naik

About the Author

Ben Frain, Senior Front-end Developer at bet365, is a widely respected CSS developer and industry thought leader. Ben is the author of two successful and widely respected books *Responsive Web Design with HTML5 and CSS3* and *Sass and Compass for Designers*, both published by *Packt Publishing*. Ben lives in Cheshire, England with his wife and two children. You can follow him on Twitter at `http://twitter.com/benfrain` and at his website (`http://benfrain.com`).

Thanks

I'd like to extend my thanks to a few people who directly or indirectly helped in getting this book written.

Firstly, Matthew Mitchell (`http://mattmitchell.co.uk`), who provided the `http://ecss.io` website design, and endures (pun intended) my constant blathering about CSS.

I'd also like to thank my work colleagues at bet365, principally Pete Griffiths (`http://twitter.com/kungfusheep`) who encouraged the development teams to make use of the ECSS approach on a grand scale.

Finally, I'd like to thank my long-suffering wife for allowing me to 'tap away' in the kitchen for countless hours in order to get this stuff out of my head.

www.PacktPub.com

For support files and downloads related to your book, please visit www.PacktPub.com.

Did you know that Packt offers eBook versions of every book published, with PDF and ePub files available? You can upgrade to the eBook version at www.PacktPub.com and as a print book customer, you are entitled to a discount on the eBook copy. Get in touch with us at service@packtpub.com for more details.

At www.PacktPub.com, you can also read a collection of free technical articles, sign up for a range of free newsletters and receive exclusive discounts and offers on Packt books and eBooks.

https://www.packtpub.com/mapt

Get the most in-demand software skills with Mapt. Mapt gives you full access to all Packt books and video courses, as well as industry-leading tools to help you plan your personal development and advance your career.

Why subscribe?

- Fully searchable across every book published by Packt
- Copy and paste, print, and bookmark content
- On demand and accessible via a web browser

Table of Contents

Preface

This is a little book that encapsulates my current thinking on how best to write and maintain CSS codebases for rapidly changing, long-lived web projects.

- There is no framework to download
- There are no requisite tools (although there are opinionated guidelines for what tooling should provide)
- Nothing is written for you

Put metaphorically, *Enduring CSS* is not giving you fish; it's teaching you how to fish.

It's a methodology for writing CSS that once implemented, will provide your project with a predictable, and easy to maintain CSS codebase.

The earliest iterations of *Enduring CSS* were first documented in August 2014, in the blog post, *Enduring CSS: writing style sheets for rapidly changing, long-lived projects* (`https://benfrain.com/enduring-css-writing-style-sheets-rapidly-changing-long-lived-projects/`).

However, the ECSS approach has developed a little since then and so this book should be considered the canonical resource on the approach.

I hope you enjoy reading it.

Ben Frain

1
Writing Styles for Rapidly Changing, Long-lived Projects

This isn't actually a book about writing CSS, as in the stuff inside the curly braces. It's a book about the organising and architecture of CSS; the parts outside the braces. It's the considerations that can be happily ignored on smaller projects but actually become the most difficult part of writing CSS in larger projects.

Terms like *CSS at scale*, or *Large-scale CSS* can seem quite nebulous. I'll try and clarify.

When people talk about *large scale CSS* or *writing CSS at scale* there can be a few possible metrics that relate to the *large* or *big* part of the description:

- It might be CSS that simply has a large file size. There's a lot of CSS output and so making changes to that codebase can be difficult, as there is so much of the code to consider.
- The CSS could be said to be *large* due to the complexity of the user interface that is being built with it. The overall file size may be smaller than the first situation but there may be a great many pieces of user interface that's codified in those styles. Considering how to effect changes across all of those visuals may be problematic.

- It might be *large CSS* simply due to the number of developers that have, are, and will be likely to touch and change the CSS codebase.

Or, it can be all the above.

Defining the problem

Enduring CSS was born from my own need to define a rational approach to writing CSS on large scale web applications.

The definition of what makes something a *web application* as opposed to merely a *web page* can be divisive so let's put that aside for now. Let's simply consider the scenario in which a new approach to writing CSS was needed.

Consider an interface that was, by necessity, densely populated with visual components; sliders, buttons, input fields etc.

In addition, consider that this interface was (and is) constantly evolving and needed to be changed rapidly. Furthermore, any changes might be made by any number of different style sheet authors.

Without a clearly defined CSS writing methodology, through the many iterations, the CSS was always out of hand. The style sheets were in a perpetual state of entropy as a result of mixed approaches, different levels of technical understanding between authors and code documentation that varied greatly in quality.

So the result was CSS that was difficult to iterate upon, hard to reason about and nobody was ever quite sure where redundancy lay. Worse still, style sheet authors lacked the confidence to remove code for fear of inadvertently effecting other parts of the application.

If you've ever inherited or worked in a team on a large CSS codebase, I'm sure some of what I'm describing will sound familiar.

Therefore, at the outset of my journey, I defined some basic needs. More simply, these were the problems that any new CSS authoring approach had to solve. Here is the list of those needs:

- To allow the easy maintenance of a large CSS codebase over time
- To allow portions of CSS code to be removed from the codebase without effecting the remaining styles
- To make it possible to rapidly iterate on any new designs

- Changing the properties and values that applied to one visual element should not unintentionally effect others
- Any solution should require minimal tooling and workflow changes to implement
- Where possible, W3C standards such as ARIA should be used to communicate state change within the user interface

In the next chapter we are going to look more specifically at these problems. However, first, an important cautionary note.

Solve your own problems

I believe in *Pin Cing Do*, which translates roughly as the *The way of pragmatic coding* (`https://benfrain.com/be-better-front-end-developer-way-of-pragmatic-coding/`). This means solving the problems you actually have. Therefore, I'll state something up front that may be obvious to some:

It may be that the problems I had were not the problems you have. As such, you should temper the advice and approach offered herein accordingly. Alternatively, consider that your needs may be better addressed by different approaches and methodologies. I'm not going to try and convince you that ECSS is necessarily the best solution in all situations. For example:

- ECSS won't give you the smallest possible CSS footprint (consider *Atomic CSS* (`http://acss.io/`) for that).
- It isn't widely used and documented (consider *BEM* (`https://en.bem.info/`) if ubiquity is a major concern).
- ECSS does not abstract styles and allow styling of elements from a bunch of specific utility classes. You should look at OOCSS and read the writing of its many advocates for that.

OK, public service announcement out of the way. Let's head on to the next chapter. This is where we'll look at the principle problems of scaling and architecting CSS for large scale projects: specificity, the cascade, isolation and selectors tied to structural elements.

2
The Problems of CSS at Scale

In the last chapter, we talked about the scenario which gave rise to the ECSS methodology. A large, CSS codebase that developers found difficult to reason about, cumbersome to work with and was littered with poorly commented and redundant code. However, no CSS codebase starts this way.

In most projects, the CSS starts out with some simple rules. At the outset, you'd have to be doing something fairly daft to make maintenance of the CSS problematic.

However, as the project grows, so too does the CSS. Requirements become more complicated. More authors get involved writing the styles. Edge cases and browser workarounds need to be authored and factored in. It's easy for things to get unruly fast.

Let's consider the growing demands on a humble widget:

- *When the widget is in the sidebar, can we reduce the font size?*
- *When we're on the home page, can the widget have a different background colour?*
- *Can we have the things inside the widget stacked vertically at larger viewports?*
- *When the widget is in the sidebar on the product page, the font colour needs to change*

Before long we need to write a whole raft of overrides to a key selector. Let's consider the selectors we might need:

```css
.widget{
    /* Base Styles */
}

aside#sidebar .widget {
    /* Sidebar specific */
}

body.home-page aside#sidebar .widget {
```

```
        /* Home page sidebar specific */
}

@media (min-width: 600px) {
    .widget {
        /* Base Styles 600px and above */
    }

    aside#sidebar .widget {
        /* Sidebar specific 600px and above */
    }

    body.home-page aside#sidebar .widget {
        /* Home page sidebar specific 600px and above */
    }
}

body.product-page .widget {
    /* Product page specific */
}

body.product-page aside#sidebar .widget {
    /* Product page sidebar specific */
}
```

There's some basic authoring problems there if this was CSS that we wanted to scale. Let's consider some of the more obvious problems in those rules now.

 The term *key selector* is used to describe the right most selector in any CSS rule. It's the selector you are attempting to affect change on.

Specificity

The first major problem when trying to scale CSS is the problem of specificity. Ordinarily, specificity is a useful thing. It allows us to introduce some form of logic in the CSS. Styles that are more specific than others get applied in the browser. Our example above demonstrates this: different rules will be applied in different eventualities (for example, when in the sidebar, we want to override the default styles).

Now, CSS selectors can be made up of ID, class, attribute & type selectors and any combination of those. With responsive designs you can throw media queries into the mix too.

However, not all selectors are created equal. The W3C describes how specificity is calculated here: `http://www.w3.org/TR/css3-selectors/#specificity`. Here is the most relevant section:

> *A selector's specificity is calculated as follows: count the number of ID selectors in the selector (= a) count the number of class selectors, attributes selectors, and pseudo-classes in the selector (= b) count the number of type selectors and pseudo-elements in the selector (= c) ignore the universal selector Selectors inside the negation pseudo-class are counted like any other, but the negation itself does not count as a pseudo-class. Concatenating the three numbers a-b-c (in a number system with a large base) gives the specificity.*

One important thing missing there is the style attribute. Information on that *elsewhere* (`https://www.w3.org/TR/css-style-attr/`) tells us that:

> *The declarations in a style attribute apply to the element to which the attribute belongs. In the cascade, these declarations are considered to have author origin and a specificity higher than any selector.*

So, a style applied in a style attribute on an element is going to be more specific than an equivalent rule in a CSS file.

Regardless, the biggest takeaway here is that ID selectors are infinitely more specific than class based selectors. This makes overriding any selector containing an ID based selector far more difficult. For example, with a widget in the sidebar this won't work:

```css
.widget {
    /* Widget in the sidebar */
}

aside#sidebar .widget {
    /* Widget in an aside element with the ID of sidebar */
}

.class-on-sidebar .widget {
    /* Why doesn't this work */
}
```

In this instance we would be applying a HTML class (`class-on-sidebar`) on the sidebar element (the aside element with the ID of sidebar) and then selecting that in the CSS lower down than the ID based selector. However, the rule still won't be applied.

Knowing what we know about specificity from the W3C specifications we can calculate the specificity of these rules.

Let's run the numbers. Left to right, the numbers after the selectors below relate to: number of inline styles, number of ID selectors, number of class selectors, and finally the number of type selectors.

selector	inline	ID	class	type
`.widget`	0	0	1	0
`aside#sidebar .widget`	0	1	1	1
`.class-on-sidebar .widget`	0	0	2	0

So you can see here that the middle selector has a greater specificity than the last. Bummer.

On a single or smaller file, this isn't that much of a big deal. We just create a more specific rule. However, if the CSS of your codebase is split across many smaller partial CSS files, finding a rule that is preventing your override from working can become an unwanted burden. Now, the problem isn't specific to ID selectors. It's more of a problem with unequally weighted selectors in the style sheets. Think of it like a heavyweight boxer pitted against a flyweight. It's not a fair contest. Creating a level playing field across the selectors used is more important than the actual selectors used.

This mis-matched soup of selectors is the crux of the specificity issue. As soon as you have a CSS codebase with hundreds of rules, any unneeded specificity starts to become a major hindrance to speedy development.

So, to conclude, specificity is a problem we need to address in an ever-growing CSS codebase.

Markup structure tied to selectors

Another practice to avoid when authoring CSS for scale is using type selectors; selectors that relate to specific markup. For example:

```
aside#sidebar ul > li a {
    /* Styles */
}
```

In this case we need to have an `a` tag inside an `li` which is a direct child of a `ul` inside an `aside` element with an ID of `sidebar` – phew!

What happens if we want to apply those styles to a `div` somewhere else? Or any other markup structure?

We've just unnecessarily tied our rule to specific markup structure. It's often quite tempting to do this, as it can seem ridiculous to add a class to something as (seemingly) trivial as an `a` or `span` tag. However, I hope once you reach the end of this book you'll be convinced to avoid the practice.

We want CSS that is as loosely coupled to structure as possible. That way, should we need to introduce an override (a more specific selector for a particular instance) we can keep things as vague as possible to get the job done. Again, get used to the idea of introducing only as much specificity as is needed.

The cascade

Typically, the cascade part of *Cascading Style Sheets* is useful. Even if specificity is very equal across the selectors used, the cascade allows equivalent rules further down the CSS to be applied over existing rules higher up.

However, in a large codebase, the cascade presents an undesirable temptation; the ability for developers to take a short cut of amending the existing CSS by simply writing more new code at the bottom of the existing CSS.

This temptation is both real and easy to identify with. It can be tempting for a number of reasons. As an example, authors more familiar with other languages that need to make changes to the CSS may lack the confidence or intimate knowledge of the CSS codebase to be able to confidently remove or amend the existing code. They therefore take the safest option and override existing rules using a more specific set of rules. At the time it seems like the responsible thing to do—just adding one or two rules as needed.

However, the problem with leaning on the cascade in this way is that over time and iteration, the CSS code becomes bloated with many redundant rules. The consumers of this CSS (the users) are downloading CSS full of cruft that their browser simply doesn't need and the maintainers of this code have more code to sift through every time they need to make sense of their codebase.

Summary

At this point, we've taken a high-level view of some of the problems that are symptomatic of a CSS codebase struggling to cope at scale. Problems such as overly specific selectors, selectors tied to specific markup structure and the temptation of leaning on the cascade and the CSS bloat that leads too.

In the next chapter, we'll look at the accepted wisdom and approaches of trying to tame large CSS codebases and consider any shortcomings they present.

3
Implementing Received Wisdom

You often don't really understand the problem until after the first time you implement a solution
-The Cathedral and the Bazaar (`http://www.catb.org/esr/writings/cathedral-b azaar/cathedral-bazaar/ar01s02.html`)

In the last chapter we considered some of the more obvious difficulties of dealing with a large CSS codebase. In this chapter, we'll consider some existing approaches for dealing with those problems.

Over the course of two years I've went on a CSS architecture and maintenance odyssey. Near the beginning of the experience I did what any sensible developer should do. I looked to see how smart people had dealt with the problem already.

CSS architectural approaches can seem like the equivalent of diet pills for the overweight. It's easy to snatch at apparent solutions, hoping they'll be exactly what you need. However, you probably don't know exactly what you need until you've tried to solve your problems at least once.

That advice applies here too. It maybe that ECSS isn't the solution to the problems you have so if you're just starting to solve your CSS issues, be sure to consider what different methodologies offer too.

At the time of my adventure, the principle approaches for dealing with CSS at scale were:

- **OOCSS (Object Orientated CSS)**, developed by *Nicole Sullivan* (http://www.stu bbornella.org/content/)
- **SMACSS (Scalable and Modular Architecture for CSS)**, developed by *Jonathan Snook* (https://snook.ca/)
- **BEM (Block Element Modifier)**, developed by *Yandex* (https://en.bem.info/)

Now, I'll tell you unashamedly right now, I've stolen elements from each. However, none of those actually solved all the problems I had.

Before we get to ECSS proper I'd like to briefly go over the advantages and disadvantages of each of the existing approaches I looked at. That way, at least when we get to ECSS you can appreciate the problems it is solving.

On OOCSS

The most widely practised, and certainly most widely lauded of the existing approaches I looked at was OOCSS. That was the first approach that I utilised when trying to wrestle my ever growing CSS codebase.

One of the principal arguments for an OOCSS approach is that it removes duplication of code and therefore results in a more maintainable CSS codebase. In essence, you build a set of CSS *Lego* pieces you can then use in your HTML/templates to quickly build out designs. The hope is that once your OOCSS styles are written they shouldn't grow (much). You re-use where possible and extend where needed.

Before we look at OOCSS I need to get some caveats out there.

1. This isn't an attack on OOCSS, Atomic CSS or any related **Single Responsibility Principle (SRP)** approaches. It's merely my argument that a different approach, depending upon your goals can offer a preferential outcome.
2. I'm not suggesting that the approach I advocate is a panacea to all CSS scaling problems. It is not (there are none).

Responsive web design, the Achilles heel of OOCSS

For me, the biggest problems with an OOCSS approach are:

- Responsive Web Design
- Frequent design changes and on-going maintenance
- An alien abstraction for new developers to learn

Let's see if I can demonstrate why I feel these issues are worth considering.

Responsive issues

I consider *Atomic CSS* (https://www.smashingmagazine.com/2013/10/challenging-css-best-practices-atomic-approach/) (not to be confused with *Atomic Design* (http://brad frost.com/blog/post/atomic-web-design/)) to represent OOCSS taken the the nth-degree. Let's consider an imaginary Atomic CSS example:

```
<div class="blk m-10 fr">Here I am</div>
```

In this OOCSS/Atomic CSS example, the visual needs of the element have been split up/abstracted into re-usable classes. One sets a block formatting context (.blk), another sets some margin (.m-10) and finally one provides a floating mechanism for the element (.fr). Un-opinionated and terse for sure.

In principle, Atomic CSS is very similar to the first architectural approach I devised.
It was called **PST!** which was an acronym for Position Structure Theme. The idea was this: there would be no semantic HTML classes/CSS selectors. Instead, every element on the page could be described by its position, structure and theme. Each new selector would just take the next available number. For example, s1, s2, s3 and on and on. It wasn't quite a class for each responsibility as is the case with Atomic CSS but it was a way of heavily abstracting stylistic needs.
Markup looked like this:
```
<div class="p1 s3 t4">Content</div>
```
Like Atomic CSS it was terse, and there was no pondering on what to call something as you authored but in practice it was hugely problematic for my needs, for the same reasons described in this chapter.

However, what happens when the viewport changes and we don't want 10px margin or the item floating?

We could of course make some classes to do things at certain breakpoints. For example, `Mplus-cc2` might change a colour at an *Mplus* breakpoint (Mplus here would be *Medium* size viewports and above). But I found this practice to be slow and laborious. Making very specific changes at certain breakpoints and tying them to a class that has to be added to the HTML seemed needlessly complex. Furthermore, you inevitably end up with a raft of SRP classes in your style sheets that are obsolete. What's the authoring mechanism for removing any cruft from the authoring styles sheets when no longer needed?

Maintenance and iteration

Let's continue with our prior example. Suppose at some point in the future, we change our product to a more progressive layout mechanism; we move from float based layouts to Flexbox based layouts. At this point, we will now have twice the maintenance burden. We will need to not only change classes in the markup/templates but also alter the CSS rules themselves (or write entirely new ones). Furthermore, using `float` is redundant with Flexbox so either we leave `.fr` alone (and so it continues to exist, needlessly in our CSS) or we make `.fr` responsible for something else such as `justify-content: flex-end`. But then what happens if we change the flex-direction of our parent at a particular viewport? Arrgggghhhh!

Hopefully you can see the inherent shortcomings of an OOCSS approach for maintenance when your designs change frequently or you need to render an entirely different layout at a different viewport?

 Atomic CSS has developed considerably since Thierry's article in Smashing Magazine back in 2013. Depending upon your goals, it may be just the thing you need, I would encourage you to check the project out at http://acss.io.

An alien abstraction for new developers

Speedily on-boarding new developers may not be an important factor for everyone. However, for situations where developers join and leave a team (or perhaps even a company) fairly regularly, it can be an important consideration. I was looking for a solution that largely allowed developers to continue writing CSS as they knew it. Forcing new developers to learn an alien abstraction can be an additional unwanted burden. In addition, it may or may not also be problematic to apply that abstraction to the template layer; after all many solutions may not even have a template layer in the traditional sense.

A pure OOCSS example

It would be fair to argue that using Atomic CSS as an example is unfair, and perhaps doesn't fairly represent OOCSS. However, trying to get a canonical example of OOCSS is difficult as there seems to be so much disparity between what CSS authors believe it is, and how it is implemented.

I'll therefore provide some further, OOCSS only, examples. I'm going to use Nicole Sullivan's original examples from her slides *Our best practices are killing us* (http://www.sli deshare.net/stubbornella/our-best-practices-are-killing-us).

I was reluctant to do this as Nicole's original examples are now very old (2009, before Responsive Web Design was even a thing) and, without wishing to speak for her, I dare say she might use a different example and approach today.

However, hopefully we can agree that the essential aims of OOCSS are *separation of structure from skin, and separating content from container* (https://github.com/stubbornella/oocss /wiki)? Assuming we are in agreement on that, it is my conviction that OOCSS is detrimental to speed of creation and codebase maintainability in certain circumstances.

In a responsive web design, there are times where the structure is the skin. Or rather, the structure does different things in different contexts, and there is no sane way to handle this with OOCSS. You however will be the judge.

Consider this OOCSS example. First the markup:

```
<div class="media attribution">
  <a href="#" class="img">
    <img src="mini.jpg" alt="Stubbornella" />
  </a>
  <div class="bd">@Stubbornella 14 minutes ago</div>
</div>
```

Now the CSS (note, I have removed some OldIE specific property/values here):

```
.media { overflow: hidden; margin: 10px; }
.media .img { float: left; margin-right: 10px; }
.media .img img { display: block; }
.media .imgExt { float: right; margin-left: 10px; }
```

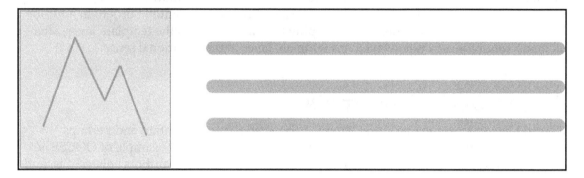

The el clasico example of OOCSS; the Media object pattern

However, maybe this media object needs to be laid out differently at a 300px wide viewport. You could set a media query to make it a column based layout in that situation. But let's say you have the same *object* in a different context at the same viewport width? And in that context, it shouldn't be in a column layout. To surmise:

1. One media object needs to be a column based layout at 300px wide (let's call this *media1*)
2. A second media object needs to be a row based layout at 300px wide (as it is within another context/container, we will call this *media2*)

Let's make a class that separates more concerns. It makes a media object a column layout at a certain viewport:

```
@media (min-width: 18.75rem) {
  .media-vp-small {
    /* Styles */
  }
}
```

That gets added to any element that needs to be a column at that viewport (*media1*) so you'll need to head over to the templates/HTML to make that change, adding the class where needed.

Furthermore, *media2* needs to have a different background colour at a larger viewport. Let's add another class to separate that concern:

```
@media (min-width: 60rem) {
  .draw-focus {
    /* Styles */
  }
}
```

Head into the HTML/template to add that style where needed.

Oh, and *media1* needs the `.img` to be wider at the larger viewport and not have the margin. We can make another class for that:

```
@media (min-width: 60rem) {
  .expand-img {
    width: 40%;
    margin-right: 0!important;
  }
}
```

Back into the HTML/templates to make that change happen.

Hopefully now, you can see where this is headed? There's a lot of Single Responsibility Principle (SRP) classes being added to facilitate the many and varied scenarios our media object needs to facilitate.

This approach was not making my large responsive code base more maintainable. In fact, quite the opposite. Whenever changes were needed it was necessary to go hunting for the particular SRP class for the specific situation and often add/remove HTML classes in the markup/templates too. Which made me ponder the question:

> *Why can't the thing, just be the thing?*

For now, you may counter with, *this is a daft example, if a design has so many eventualities, it should be normalised*. At which point I would counter that it shouldn't be necessary to. Those tasked with coding the front-end shouldn't need to hobble a designers creativity just because it makes their code less predictable. They should be able to code out a new design simply and easily without concerning themselves about how the new component/module/thing may impact others.

Trying to prevent visual changes to a project merely because they make our codebase difficult to maintain and reason about is not a defensible stance. We should be able to build out any new visual treatment with speed and predictability without fear of inadvertently affecting other areas of the project.

When I've used OOCSS to tackle my needs, my speed to build new visuals decreased and the amount of SRP classes increased; often a class got used just once or twice on an entire project. Even with a considered naming convention for SRP classes, remembering the correct class name for a particular need can require constant mental juggling.

When using OOCSS on a rapidly changing project I also found that after some time, I found it incredibly frustrating to *unpick* these abstract classes when changes were needed. I was having to make many very similar abstract classes when they were seldom actually used. Utility classes like `w10`, `w15`, `w20`, `w25` etc for different width percentages seemed like a good idea and an obvious abstraction to make but they ultimately proved useless and problematic to iterate designs with (back to the problem of things needing to do different things in different contexts).

My first big lesson when employing OOCSS therefore was the same lesson that the fine fellow *Kaelig Deloumeau-Prigent* (`http://www.kaelig.fr/`) learnt in his time working on large CSS codebases at the BBC and The Guardian newspaper:

> *Two years ago I wrote a book where I was preaching DRY code, but after working on enduring projects, it's decoupling that became more important to me.*

On large, rapidly changing projects, being able to easily decouple visual modules from the project is incredibly important for ongoing maintenance and OOCSS didn't facilitate this need well.

SMACSS

SMACSS, which stands for Scalable Modular Architecture for CSS, is detailed fully in *Jonathan Snook's book on the subject* (`https://smacss.com/`). I'm not going into detail about SMACSS here as I think you should go and check that book out for yourself. Reading SMACSS gave me plenty to chew over as I faced my own challenges and I certainly took things, such as how to think about state changes, from it. However, I will detail why SMACSS didn't work for me.

Again, like my caveat regarding my opinions on OOCSS, this isn't a critique of SMACSS. It's simply highlighting the parts that didn't work for me and why I felt it failed to solve my own problems. SMACSS has clearly defined terminology and concepts for the visual aspects of a website. It therefore prescribes base, layout, modules and optional theme rules/files to support these definitions. For example, consider this suggested file structure:

```
+-layout/
| +-grid.scss
| +-alternate.scss
+-module/
| +-callout.scss
| +-bookmarks.scss
| +-btn.scss
| +-btn-compose.scss
+-base.scss
+-states.scss
+-site-settings.scss
+-mixins.scss"
```

Excerpt From: Jonathan Snook. Scalable and Modular Architecture for CSS.

While these definitions make perfect sense in many scenarios, they didn't for mine. I wanted an approach that was looser, an approach that didn't make me need to consider fitting what I needed to build into those visual definitions; the applications I was building and maintaining often defied adherence to those definitions.

BEM

BEM is a methodology developed by the developers at `http://yandex.ru`.

The key thing I took from BEM is just how much a naming convention can buy you when it comes to CSS maintenance.

 If you are interested in reading more about BEM, the canonical resource is `http://en.bem.info`. For a good explanation of where it all began I recommend starting here: `https://en.bem.info/method/history`

Again, like SMACSS, I'm not going to attempt to fully explain the ins and outs of BEM methodology. However, I will give you the *elevator pitch* explanation of the key points. The BEM methodology works around the notion that key areas of a page can be defined as **Blocks**. In turn, those key areas are made up of Elements. We can then represent the relationship between the Block and its Elements in the way we name things. Consider the OOCSS media object example from before. In a BEM approach we might use classes like this:

```
<div class="media">
  <a href="#" class="media__img">
    <img class="media__headshot" src="mini.jpg"
    alt="Stubbornella" />
  </a>
  <div class="media__attribution">@Stubbornella 14 minutes
  ago</div>
</div>
```

What's so useful about this naming scheme is that it clearly communicates a relationship between the elements and the block they belong to. Plus, away from the HTML, if we came across a selector like this in the CSS:

```
.media__headshot {

}
```

We instantly know that this is a Element called **headshot** that lives inside a Block called **media**. This namespacing a component as part of something else helps to isolate styles and prevent the applied styles from *leaking* out – one of my major bug-bears with OOCSS. This was definitely a step in the right direction for the problems I was trying to solve.

BEM also has the notion of *modifiers*. A modifier is something that gets added to the Block to modify its appearance. Suppose we wanted to theme our media object differently in a different scenario. BEM facilitates it like this:

```
<div class="media media_dark">
  <a href="#" class="media__img">
    <img class="media__headshot" src="mini.jpg"
    alt="Stubbornella" />
  </a>
  <div class="media__attribution">@Stubbornella 14 minutes
  ago</div>
</div>
```

The BEM documents dictate the use of a single underscore character to identify a Modifier for a Block. This modifier class must always be used alongside the block name. For example, you must do this:

```
<div class="media media_dark">
```

And not this:

 <div class="media_dark">

I see the value in using modifiers in this manner but it proved problematic for me. Often the things I was styling needed to behave differently in a more traditional manner. Perhaps visuals needed to display differently depending upon the context they were being used, or if another class was being added above it in the DOM. Or due to certain media query conditions, or indeed any combination of those scenarios. I needed a way to author styles that was pragmatic enough to deal with the non-ideal situations that occurred. Some way to keep some sanity in the authoring style sheets no matter what was thrown at them.

Summary

Of all the existing CSS methodologies I looked at, I took the most from BEM. There is much to appreciate in BEM:

- All elements get the same specificity; a class is added to all the elements.
- There is no use of type selectors so HTML structure isn't tightly coupled to the styles.
- It's easy to reason about what the parent of an element is, whether viewing the DOM tree in the browser developer tools or the CSS in a code editor.

However, the use of modifiers didn't really fit my needs. Although perhaps it wasn't preferable, my reality was that often I would need to override styles on a Block (in BEM parlance) depending upon some eventuality above it or by the side of it in the DOM.

For example, in the scenario where existing logic is already determined in an application, there may be a scenario where a class like `contains2columns` would be added above the item in question in the DOM and I would need to style changes based upon that, as opposed to changes directly upon the Block in question.

With BEM I couldn't find a clear way of understanding how that eventuality should be handled. Or how I could contain those kinds of overrides in the authoring style sheets. I wanted to define items and encapsulate all the eventualities that may occur on a particular item.

I also found the syntax confusing to reason over when glancing at classes. The differentiation between the way modifiers were written and the way elements were written was negligible. This would be an easy fix but it was still something that bugged me about it.

Finally, I realised I needed something extra. I wanted the ability to communicate and facilitate different contexts for a module. When a *thing* was created by the same piece of logic but could be used and styled differently in different contexts, I wanted a means of communicating that.

From SMACSS the main thing I found useful was dealing with state. I liked the declarative manner in which classes like `is-pressed` or attributes `.btn[data-state=pressed]` clearly communicated the state of elements.

OOCSS turned out to be the antithesis of what I needed. Whilst I appreciate what OOCSS can offer, it wasn't the solution to the problems I had. I didn't want to create a Lego box of styles that authors could use to build up visuals in a DOM/template. The abstractions OOCSS facilitated were inherently *leaky* which made maintenance problematic (change the value in one rule and you may inadvertently effect many elements), it was also difficult to find ways of dealing with varying viewports, for all the reasons already explained and the additional abstraction added further complications when on-boarding new developers.

Ultimately, by trying and failing, to varying degrees, with each of these existing solutions I finally fully understood my problems. Now it was time to tailor a bespoke solution. To paraphrase Pablo Picasso:

> *Good coders copy, great coders steal* **Pablo Picasso** *(sort of – sorry Pablo)*

Walk with me.

4

Introducing the ECSS Methodology

In the last chapter we considered existing CSS methodologies, and where, for your humble authors needs, they fell short.

I'm not about to try and convince you that the Enduring CSS approach is the *Alpha and the Omega*. However, it does have different strengths and aims than the existing approaches. Therefore, even if taking it wholesale doesn't appeal, I'd hope there may be something you can borrow to solve your own issues.

Highlights of ECSS:

- It gains maintainability by isolating each visual pattern
- File size remains minimal over long periods of time by virtue of the fact that you can cut out sections/features/components with impunity
- Rules are *self-quarantining*
- Class names/selectors can communicate context, originating logic and variation
- All rules, their effects and reach are entirely predictable

When I first wrote about Enduring CSS I was expecting a backlash of sorts. At that time (August 2014), no-one was really advocating what I was suggesting. Received wisdom for scaling CSS was to abstract visual patterns, normalise designs as much as possible and DRY out code. *Enduring CSS* is, in some ways, the antithesis of these beliefs.

In this chapter, we won't be dealing with the specific technical detail of ECSS, such as naming conventions, tooling, authoring and organisation. We'll be covering those subjects in detail in future chapters. Instead, we will be looking at the broad aims and benefits of the approach as it compares to other approaches.

 In case you aren't aware of the acronym, DRY stands for Don't Repeat Yourself, a popular goal when coding so that logic is only written once in a codebase to provide a single source of truth.

Before we get into this, I think it may help to clarify the terminology that will be used. The terms used to define the visual parts of a page are known by different names in different approaches. There's nothing revelatory in what I'm suggesting or the terms I'm using, it's just important we're all on the same page before we get into this.

Defining terminology

I'm using the term *module* to designate an area of functionality and/or the code that creates it. To exemplify, the header of a website could be considered a module. The header module would, in turn, be made up of other smaller pieces of functionality. For example, drop-down menus or search boxes. These nested pieces of functionality would be defined as components. Finally, our smallest *items* would be the child nodes that make up a component or module.

So, to reiterate:

- A **module** is the widest, visually identifiable, individual section of functionality
- **Components** are the nested pieces of functionality that are included within a module
- **Child nodes** are the individual parts that go to make up a component (typically nodes in the DOM)

For brevity, for what follows, when I'm referring to modules, it could be a module or component. The difference from a ECSS authoring perspective is unimportant.

The problems ECSS solves

My primary goal with ECSS was to isolate styles as opposed to abstracting them.

Ordinarily, it makes sense to create CSS classes that are abstractions of common functionality. The benefit being that they can then be re-used and re-applied on many varied elements. That's sound enough in principle. The problem is, on larger and more complicated user interfaces, it becomes impossible to make even minor tweaks and amendments to those abstractions without inadvertently effecting things you didn't intend to.

A guiding principle with ECSS therefore was to isolate styles to the intended target.

Depending upon your goals, even at the cost of repetition, isolation can buy you greater advantages; allowing for predictable styling and simple decoupling of styles.

A further advantage of isolating styles is that designers can be encouraged to bring whatever they need making, without necessarily feeling encumbered by existing visual patterns. Every new module that needs to be coded can be a *greenfield*. I found that I could code out designs far faster when starting from scratch than attempting to build them from any number of vague abstractions.

Dealing with specificity

I also wanted to negate issues surrounding specificity. To this ends, I adopted the widely used approach of insisting all selectors used a single (or as close to that ideal as possible) class-based selector.

> *If you're having CSS problems I feel bad for you son, I got 99 problems but specificity ain't one*
> —https://twitter.com/benfrain/status/537339394706141184

Furthermore, structural HTML elements (with the exception of pseudo-elements) are NEVER referenced in the style sheets as type selectors. In addition ID selectors are completely avoided in ECSS. Not because ID selectors are bad per se, but because we need a level playing field of selector strength.

Changes to components are handled via simple overrides. However, the way they are handled from an authoring perspective makes them easy to manage and reason about.

Suppose you have an element that needs to be a different width if it is within a certain container – easy peasy, we don't need to be draconian in the manner an override can happen. We don't need a modifier applied to that specific element. We can handle typical and very loose override scenarios but manage them confidently. You would write it like this in the authoring style sheets:

```
.my-Module_Component {
    width: 100%;
    /* If in the sidebar */
    .sw-Sidebar & {
        width: 50%;
    }
}
```

And it would yield this CSS:

```
.my-Module_Component {
  width: 100%;
}

.sw-Sidebar .my-Module_Component {
  width: 50%;
}
```

This may seem like a subtle benefit. After all, we may be authoring things a little differently by nesting the overrides, but the net result is typical CSS; an element that gets different styles based upon a different and more specific selector.

 The use of the ampersand symbol within a nesting context to denote the parent selector is a convention borrowed from the *Sass* (http://sass-lan g.com/) language.

However, by adopting this approach, from an authoring perspective, we create a *single source of truth* for each key selector. Everything that will ever make a change to that key selector is nested inside that opening set of curly braces. Furthermore, that key selector will never be defined as a root rule anywhere else in the entire codebase.

Different interpretations of DRY

I wasn't convinced that the goal of DRY code that other CSSers were pursuing and extolling the virtues of, was the same kind of DRY code I wanted. To explain that a little more – I didn't care much about repeated values and pairs across my rules, which is what most people were concentrating on DRYing out. What I cared about was key selectors not being repeated in the codebase. Key selectors were my *single source of truth* and that was the area I wanted to DRY out. To that ends, with ECSS, an authoring convention is enforced that prevents a key selector being defined more than once project-wide. We will get into that in much more detail in `Chapter 8`, *The Ten Commandments of Sane Style Sheets*.

This is !important

If on the odd occasion the presence of one override isn't enough, we can make use of `!important`.

You will likely be aware that using `!important` in CSS is generally frowned upon. Here's what MDN has to say about `!important`:

> *When an !important rule is used on a style declaration, this declaration overrides any other declaration made in the CSS, wherever it is in the declaration list. Although, !important has nothing to do with specificity, using !important is bad practice because it makes debugging hard since you break the natural cascading in your style sheets*
> —`https://developer.mozilla.org/en-US/docs/Web/CSS/Specificity`

However, when events beyond our control mess with our styles (e.g. a 3rd party CSS file loaded on the page) and we need some clout, I embrace !important. Here's an example of a state change that is receiving some extra welly from !important:

```
[aria-expanded="true"] & {
    transform: translate3d(0, -$super-height,
    0)!important;
}
```

I'll be honest, I really don't lose much sleep over using `!important` when it is needed. Thanks to all overrides being localised to their parent selector in the authoring style sheets, the occasional use of `!important` presents no problems in ECSS.

Embracing repetition

Before we get much further, I think it's important to deal with a possible *elephant in the room*. I need to try and convince you that eliminating repetition of properties and values across files may not buy as much, from a maintenance perspective, as a solid and contained set of modules that are easy to remove from a codebase as needed.

The ECSS approach embraces repetition of properties and values in the CSS.

With ECSS, every single visual module or component is written with a micro-namespace to provide isolation from other modules and components. Here is a typical example of an authored ECSS rule (the authoring syntax is very similar to Sass, but typically facilitated by PostCSS):

```
.ip-SubHeader_Wrapper {
    @mixin Headline;
    align-items: center;
    /* We want the subheader hidden by default at the
    smallest sizes */
    display: none;
    font-size: $text12;
    background-color: $color-grey-54;
    border-bottom: 1px solid color($color-grey-54 a(.5));
    min-height: $size-fine-quadruple;
    @media (min-width: $SM) {
        display: inline-block;
    }
    @media (min-width: $M) {
        display: flex;
        background-color: $color-grey-a7;
        color: $color-grey-54;
        font-size: $text13;
        min-height: 1.5rem;
        border-bottom: 1px solid $color-grey-54;
        border-top: 1px solid $color-grey-33;
    }
    /* However, even on mobile, if the SubHeader Wrapper
    is in section 1, we want to see it */
    .ip-Classification_Header-1 & {
        display: flex;
    }
}
```

Those inclined towards OOCSS and Atomic CSS methodologies may look at that and shudder. Things like `color` and `font-size` are declared in most components. The `@mixin Headline` mixin generates a sizeable chunk of CSS to designate a particular font stack too. So, yes, there's repetition of properties and values.

However, the positives:

- It's verbose yet it relies on no inheritance of styles.
- It's generally context agnostic (save for the size context of where it is placed), any media queries that affect this component are defined within this single set of curly braces.
- A key selector like this is written once and once only. When this key selector needs to change, you only need to look in this one place.
- Writing rules with all overrides nested within creates a sort of micro-cascade. Where ordinarily overrides could be anywhere in the CSS, adhering to this method confines them to a very specific area. It then becomes far easier to reason about specificity as it relates to the rule

Zero component abstractions

With ECSS, if a component needs to be made that is similar, yet subtly different to an existing component, we would not abstract or extend from this existing component. Instead, a new one would be written.

Yes, I'm serious.

Even if 95% of it is the same.

The benefit of this is that each component is then independent and isolated. One can exist without the other. One can change however it needs to, independently from the other. Despite their apparent aesthetic similarity at the outset, they can mutate as needed with no fear of infecting or tainting any other similar looking component. To extend the biological metaphor, we have gained components that are *self-quarantining* by virtue of their unique namespace.

A further analogy: A BMW 3 series has a lot in common with a BMW 5 series. But they are not the same. They may share some/many parts (the equivalent of CSS property and value combinations) but that doesn't make them the same. Their differences define them. They cannot be made of exactly the same parts because there is something inherently different about them. I'd argue it is the same case with modules and components defined with ECSS. The CSS language is the abstraction. The property/value pairs of CSS already mean we can build what we want from individual parts.

The cost of repetition?

To fully reap the benefits of ECSS you need to be comfortable with the property and value repetition it creates. At this point, you may believe me deluded. With all this duplication, how can this ECSS approach be a viable option? I'll address that concern with one word: gzip.

OK, I lied. I'd like to qualify that further.

gzip is incredibly efficient at compressing repetitive strings

I was curious what *real world* difference the verbosity of repeated property/value pairs in an approach like ECSS actually made? An experiment:

The resultant CSS file of a ECSS based project I was working on, when gzipped (as it would be served *over the wire*), was 42.9 KB. That's a significantly sized CSS file.

The most common and verbose patterns that could be abstracted from this style sheet to an OOCSS class was a couple of Flex based rules that were used abundantly throughout to vertically centre content within their container. They were even more verbose thanks to the fact that there was considerable code added by *Autoprefixer* (https://github.com/postcss/autoprefixer) to enable support on older devices. For example, the resultant CSS for defining flex layout was:

```
.flex {
    display: -webkit-box;
    display: -webkit-flex;
    display: -ms-flexbox;
    display: flex;
```

```
}
```

In the test style sheet, those four lines of CSS were repeated **193** times.

That was only half of it. Many of those items needed aligning too. That required this in the CSS too:

```
.flex-center {
    -webkit-box-align: center;
    -webkit-align-items: center;
    -ms-flex-align: center;
    align-items: center;
}
```

That block was repeated **117** times. Doesn't seem like any better reason to abstract to an OOCSS class, right? That must be causing some serious bloat right there?

Not so fast, Batman!

If those blocks of code were removed and the file re-gzipped, the CSS file size dropped to 41.9 KB.

Extracting the most common and verbose visual pattern to an OOCSS class saved just 1 KB of CSS over the wire. And despite just a 1 KB saving in the CSS, factor in that if abstracting those styles to Single Responsibility Classes (e.g. `.flex` and `.flex-center`), it would also be necessary to litter the HTML with the relevant OOCSS classes to get the visual effect back.

Does that make Single Responsibility Classes worth it?

Given that no other property combination had anything like that sort of verbosity and repetition, from a file size perspective, certainly not in my book. It would cost a lot of development agility (remember abstraction makes authoring and iteration slower as its necessary to change both templates and CSS) and responsive flexibility (what if I want this thing to do something different in a different viewport) for a minor saving in CSS file size. It's the CSS equivalent of *robbing Peter to pay Paul*.

Let me be quite clear. Despite the efficacy of gzip, if your priority is having the smallest possible CSS file size, ECSS isn't your best choice.

Instead, go take a look at *Atomic CSS* (`http://acss.io/`). Its creators are smart people, indeed, *Thierry Koblentz* (`http://www.cssmojo.com/`) is one of the smartest CSSers I know of. I'm sure ACSS will serve your needs well.

On the other hand, the priorities of ECSS are developer ergonomics (understandable class-naming conventions), easy maintainability (styles organised by component and simple to delete) and style encapsulation (namespacing prevents leaky abstractions).

Different problems, different solution.

Summary

I hope I've given you enough to consider that obsessing over repeated property values and pairs might not be the best use of your time if you are trying to create maintainable style sheets. In the next chapter, besides looking at the benefits of the ECSS naming convention, I'll also be arguing that a sound organisational approach to project maintenance will generate far leaner style sheets in the long term than class abstraction and re-use.

5
File Organisation and Naming Conventions

In the last chapter we took a high-level overview of the design considerations of ECSS. In this chapter we will start digging a little deeper into how we actually get started using ECSS.

Two cornerstones of making ECSS work for you are adhering to the file organisation and class naming convention principles. Let's look at each of these aspects next.

Project organisation

If we want to facilitate the easy removal of code from our website/application, we need to think about the way we organise the files that make up our project. Typically, when building websites, particularly web applications, it's useful to think in terms of modules or components; definable sections of the user interface. These modules might be defined primarily by visual areas or perhaps due to the files that generate them. Either way, taking the time to consider the organisation of these modules is well worth the time investment.

Ordinarily, it's a common practice to split the files in a project by technology type.

Consider this basic folder structure:

```
my-project/
- html/
- js/
- css/
```

In each of these folders you might name related files. For example:

```
my-project/
- html/
    - v2ShoppingCart.html
- js/
    - v2ShoppingCart.js
- css/
    - v2ShoppingCart.css
```

The rub though is that beyond a certain point, even giving the files related names, it's difficult to reason about how each style sheet, logic file and template in a project relate. There might be 80+ CSS partials in the `css` folder and 50+ template stubs in the `html` folder.

 I recognise the reality is that the *view* part of a website or application is usually generated by any number of different technologies such as Ruby, PHP, .NET or even JavaScript – rather than vanilla HTML.

It then becomes increasingly necessary to rely on *find* in the text editor/IDE to find any templates that a certain class is being used on. The same is true in reverse; *find* is needed to locate the partial(s) that contain the styles needed for a certain module template.

This structure doesn't make things unworkable, just inefficient and it typically requires a little mental orientation to remember what goes with what.

While not essential for ECSS, it's generally preferable that rather than organise by technology type, files are organised and grouped by visual or logical component. So, instead of this:

```
html/
- shopping-cart-template.html
- callouts-template.html
- products-template.html

js/
- shopping-cart-template.js
- callouts-template.js
- products-template.js

css/
- shopping-cart-template.css
- callouts-template.css
- products-template.css
```

We aim for something like this:

```
shopping-cart-template/
    - shopping-cart.html
    - shopping-cart.css
    - shopping-cart.js

callouts-template/
    - callouts.html
    - callouts.js
    - callouts.css

products-template/
    - products.html
    - products.js
    - products.css
```

At first glance this may seem like a seemingly unimportant distinction but it brings important benefits.

The code for each component becomes physically self-enclosed. Then, on our enduring project, when features need changing or are deprecated, all associated code for that module (styles, view logic (HTML), and JS) can be easily updated/removed.

Due credit

Nicolas Gallagher (`http://nicolasgallagher.com/`) is always ahead of the game when it comes to thinking about CSS implementations at scale and I took and adapted large elements (specifically code organisation by component) of this approach from his work. I'd been name-spacing components for some time (and I'm therefore claiming pseudo multiple discovery) but the approach of organising code by component is taken entirely from *hearing him talk* (`https://www.youtube.com/watch?v=m0oMH G6ZXvo`) on this matter.

With the exception of intentionally *global* CSS, all code that relates to the presentation of a component or module should be included in the partials that sit alongside the HTML/JS of that component.

Although you may not like it, there's always a degree of global CSS needed; at the very least a simple set of reset or normalise styles for example.

When a module is deprecated, all files associated with it can be easily removed from the codebase in one go; just delete the folder containing the module.

Just to be crystal clear, consider this folder structure for our imagined `ShoppingCart` component:

```
ShoppingCart/
    - ShoppingCart.js
    - ShoppingCart.css
```

Now suppose we create a new shopping cart:

```
v2ShoppingCart/
    - v2ShoppingCart.js
    - v2ShoppingCart.css
```

As soon as our `v2` shopping cart is finished, it's easy to remove the code for the prior version from our code base; we just delete the folder `ShoppingCart` containing our old code.

When same folder organisation isn't possible

It may not be possible or preferable to contain style sheets, assets, and application logic within the same folder.

In that situation, the next best choice is to mimic the structure of the logic. To exemplify. Suppose the logic for a component is stored in a folder structure like this:

```
src/app/v2ShoppingCart/v2ShoppingCart.js
```

We should mimic this structure as far as possible. On any sizeable application this will make locating related files easier. So we might do this – matching the folder hierarchy of the logic file as much as possible:

```
src/app/css/v2ShoppingCart/v2ShoppingCart.css
```

Same parent folder should definitely be considered the *gold* standard when using ECSS but in the absence of that, mimicking the structure of the logic files should provide some of the benefits.

With a concrete idea of how to organise the files within our project, let's turn to the principle way in which we can convey additional meaning and developer convenience to our selectors/classes.

Naming classes and selectors with ECSS

Back in `Chapter 3`, *Implementing Received Wisdom*, I recognised the benefits that the BEM approach of naming CSS selectors gave us. Naming a block and then naming any child elements in relation to that block created a namespace for the child elements.

Namespacing the CSS of a module creates a form of isolation. By preventing name collisions with other elements, chunks of CSS can be more easily moved from one environment to another (from prototype to production for example). It's also far less likely that a change of styles on one selector would inadvertently affect another.

There are a number of other approaches to solve the name collision problem. For example, if you are building an application with the popular *React* (`https://facebook.github.io/react/`) framework, consider *Radium* (`https://github.com/FormidableLabs/radium`) which will inline the styles for each node so you can effectively serve no CSS at all. Naturally, there are trade-offs such as a lack of caching and no way to add reset styles but it it certainly solves the issue at hand. In addition, when not building with React, consider *CSS Modules* (`https://github.com/css-modules/css-modules`). While requiring more involved tooling than ECSS it means you could forgo having to think about naming things altogether as it creates CSS scoped for you. Read *more about that here* (`http s://medium.com/seek-ui-engineering/the-end-of-global-css-90d2a 4a06284`).

ECSS takes the notion of selector namespacing and turns it *up to 11* (`https://en.wikipedia .org/wiki/Up_to_eleven`). Selectors are effectively namespaced in two ways:

- A micro namespace: usually used to designate context but can also indicate a parent module
- The module's own namespace: usually the name of the logic file that created the element in question

Let's look at these in more detail. The *micro* namespace is a simple 2–3 letter namespace for each module. Building a shopping cart? Try `. sc-` as your micro namespace. Building the next version of that same shopping cart? That'll be `. sc2-` then. It's just enough to isolate your component styles and allow the styles to be more self documenting. Let's consider a more involved example.

 When it comes to naming things, different things will make sense in different projects. While ECSS can happily adapt to different approaches, I would recommend a consistent approach on each project.

For example, suppose the micro namespace was being used to convey the parent or origin of the logic that created it. Back to our shopping cart example. We might have a file called `ShoppingCart.php` that contains all the logic relating to our imaginary shopping cart. We could therefore use `sc-` as an abbreviation of that file name so we know that any elements that begin with that namespace relate to the shopping cart and are rendered by that related file.

In this case, we would then have selectors like:

- `sc-Title` : The title of the shopping cart
- `sc-RemoveBtn` : A button that removes an item from the shopping cart

Here the selectors are quite compact–aesthetically pleasing if a selector can even be described in that way. However, suppose we have a shopping cart which can live in multiple contexts. A mini cart view and a full page view. In that instance we might decide to use the micro namespace to convey context. For example:

- `mc-ShoppingCart_Title` : The title of the shopping cart, generated by the file `ShoppingCart` when in the *mini cart* view/context.
- `mc-ShoppingCart_RemoveBtn` : The remove button of the shopping cart, generated by the file `ShoppingCart` when in the *mini cart* view/context.

Neither of these is the one true way. Part of ECSS philosophy is that while some core principles are essential, it can adapt to differing needs. Generally speaking, for smaller scale use cases, the former approach is fine. However, despite the comparative verbosity of the selectors in the second approach, it is the most resilient and self-documenting. With the second approach you know context, the file that generated the selector (and therefore the module it belongs to) and the element it relates to.

There is more specific information about applying ECSS conventions to web applications and visual modules in `Chapter 7`, *Applying ECSS to Your Website or Application*.

Reiterating the benefits

As namespaced modules and components are almost guaranteed to not leak into one another, it makes it incredibly easy to build out and iterate on new designs. It affords a hitherto un-thinkable blanket of impunity. Just make a new partial file for the thing you are building, assign a suitable micro-namespace and module name and write your styles, confident in the fact you won't be adversely affecting anything you don't want to. If the new thing you are building doesn't work out, you can just delete the partial file, also confident that you won't be removing the styles for something else. CSS authoring and maintenance confidence – finally!

Source order becomes unimportant

As our rules are now isolated, it makes the order of rules in a style sheet unimportant. This benefit becomes essential when working on a large-scale project. In these scenarios it is often preferable for partial files to be assembled in any order. With rules isolated from each other, this is simple. With our *self-quarantined* rules, it makes file globbing of partial styles sheets simple and risk free. With some basic tooling in place you can compile all the CSS partials within a module in one fell swoop like this:

```
@import "**/*.css";
```

No more writing @import statements for every partial in a project and worrying about the order they are in.

We will talk more about file globbing in `Chapter 9`, *Tooling for an ECSS Approach*.

Anatomy of the ECSS naming convention

As the naming of items is so useful and essential to achieving our goals, the following section documents the naming convention of ECSS in more detail. Think of this like a *Haynes manual* (`https://haynes.co.uk/catalog/manuals-online`) for your CSS selectors.

Here's a breakdown of an ECSS selector:

```
.namespace-ModuleOrComponent_ChildNode-variant {}
```

To illustrate the separate sections, here is the anatomy of that selector with the sections delineated with square brackets:

```
.[namespace][-ModuleOrComponent][_ChildNode][-variant]
```

 With more than a couple of developers on a project I'd recommended that commits to a codebase are automatically rejected that don't follow the ECSS naming pattern. Some information on necessary tooling to facilitate this is covered in `Chapter 9`, *Tooling for an ECSS Approach*.

Explanation of selector sections

Let's go back over the various parts of the ECSS selector and the allowed character types:

- `Namespace`: This is a **required** part of every selector. The micro-namespace should be all lowercase/train-case. It is typically an abbreviation to denote context or originating logic.
- `Module or Component`: This is a upper camel case/pascal case. It should always be preceded by a hyphen character (-).
- `ChildNode`: This is an optional section of the selector. It should be upper camel case/pascal case and preceded by an underscore (_).
- `Variant`: This is a further optional section of the selector. It should be written all lowercase/train-case.

Using this syntax, each part of a class name can be logically discerned from another. More information on what these sections are and how they should be employed follows:

Namespace

As discussed above, the first part of a HTML class/CSS selector is the micro namespace (all lowercase/train-case). The namespace is used to prevent collisions and provide some soft isolation for easier maintenance of rules.

Module or Component

This is the visual module or piece of logic that created the selector. It should be written in upper camel case. I've seen ECSS applied to great effect when the module or component directly references the name of the file that creates it. For example, a file called `CallOuts.js` could have a selector such as `sw-CallOuts` (the `sw-` micro namespace here used to denote it would be used *Site Wide*). This removes any ambiguity for future developers as to the origin point of this element.

Child node

If something UpperCamelCase is preceded by an underscore (_) it is a child node of a module or component.

For example:

```
.sc-Item_Header {}
```

Here, _Header is indicating that this node is the `Header` child node of the `Item` module or component that belongs to the `sc` namespace (and if it it were a component, that namespace could indicate the parent module).

Variant

If something is all lowercase/train-case and not the first part of a class name it is a variant flag. The variant flag is reserved for eventualities where many variants of a selector need to be referenced. Suppose we have a module that needs to display a different background image depending upon what category number has been assigned to it. We might use the variant indicator like this:

```
.sc-Item_Header-bg1 {} /* Image for category 1 */.
sc-Item_Header-bg2 {} /* Image for category 2 */.
sc-Item_Header-bg3 {} /* Image for category 3 */
```

Here the `-bg3` part of the selector indicates that this. `sc-Item_Header` is the category 3 version (and can therefore have an appropriate style assigned).

Doubling up on ECSS selectors

Our previous example indicates a perfect situation where it would be appropriate to use two classes on the element. One to assign default styles and another to set specifics of a variant.

Consider this markup:

```
<div class="sc-Item_Header sc-Item_Header-bg1">
    <!-- Stuff -->
</div>
```

Here we would set the universal styles for the element with `sc-Item_Header` and then the styles specific to the variant with `sc-Item_Header-bg1`. There's nothing revolutionary about this approach, I'm just documenting it here to make it clear there is nothing in the ECSS approach that precludes this practice.

Summary

We've covered a lot of detail in this chapter. The two main areas we looked at were how to organise the language files of our project so that they can be more easily maintained and how to name HTML classes/CSS selectors in ECSS so that the class of an element in the DOM can tell us everything we need to know about its origin, purpose and intended context. We also had a detailed look at the accepted syntax for ECSS selectors: where and how to apply casing differences to delineate different parts of the selector. So far, we have only concerned ourself with static elements. In the next chapter we will look at how ECSS deals with the changing state of a website or application.

6

Dealing with State Changes in ECSS

In the last chapter we considered project organisation and how to understand and apply the ECSS class naming conventions. In this chapter we will move our focus to how ECSS deals with active interfaces and how we can facilitate style changes in a rationale and accessible manner.

The majority of web applications need to deal with states.

First let's just crystallise what we mean by *states*. Consider some examples:

- A user clicks a button
- A value in an interface is updated
- An area of an interface is disabled
- A widget in the interface is busy
- An entered value exceeds allowable values
- A section of the application starts containing live data

All these eventualities can be defined as **state changes**. State changes that we typically need to communicate to the user. As such they are changes that need to be communicated to the DOM, and subsequently our style sheets need some sane way of catering to these needs.

How can we define these state changes in a consistent and considered manner?

How ECSS used to handle state change

Back in `Chapter 3`, *Implementing Received Wisdom*, I related how much I liked the SMACSS approach of communicating state. For example:

```
.has-MiniCartActive {}
```

Indicates that on, or somewhere below this node, the *mini cart* is active.

Another example:

```
.is-ShowingValue {}
```

This would communicate that the Component or one within it is showing some value (that was previously hidden).

Historically, that was how I communicated state when applying ECSS. I used a micro-namespaced class, in addition to any existing classes on the node to communicate this state. For example:

```
.is-Suspended {}
.is-Live {}
.is-Selected {}
.is-Busy {}
```

A node using these classes in the DOM might look like this:

```
<button class="co-Button is-Selected">Old Skool Button</button>
```

Historically, changing a class in the DOM, especially near the root of the DOM has been discouraged. Doing so invalidates the render tree meaning the browser has to perform a whole bunch of re-calculation. However, things are improving. Recent work by Antii Koivisto in WebKit (which powers iOS and Safari browsers) means that such changes are now *near optimal*. Interested parties can read the WebKit Changeset for class changes here: `http://trac.webkit.org/changeset/196383` and attribute selectors, such as `aria-*` here: `http://trac.webkit.org/changeset/196629`

Switching to WAI-ARIA

However, having researched ARIA a little for another book, (*Responsive Web Design with HTML5 and CSS3* in case you are interested) it struck me that if this information has to go in the DOM purely for styling hooks, it may as well lift a little more weight while it's there.

These same styling hooks can actually be placed in the DOM as *WAI-ARIA* (`https://www.w3.org/TR/wai-aria/`) states. The `States and Properties` section of WAI-ARIA describes the W3C's standardised manner in which to communicate states and properties to assistive technology within an application. In the opening section of the abstract description for WAI-ARIA, it contains this:

> *These semantics are designed to allow an author to properly convey user interface behaviors (sic) and structural information to assistive technologies in document-level markup*

While the specification is aimed at helping communicate state and properties to users with disability (via assistive technology) it serves the need of ECSS beautifully. What a great result! We get to improve the accessibility of our web application, while also gaining a clearly defined, well considered lexicon for communicating the states we need in our application logic. Here's the prior example re-written with aria to communicate state:

```
<button class="co-Button" aria-selected="true">Old Skool Button</button>
```

Class handles the aesthetics of the button. The `aria-*` attribute communicates the state (if any) of that node or its descendants.

In JavaScript application land, the only change needed is shifting from `classList` amendments for state changes to `setAttribute` amendments. For example, to set our `button` attribute:

```
button.setAttribute("aria-selected", "true");
```

 Be aware that separating concerns in this manner does require an additional *touchpoint* in your JavaScript. If you absolutely, positively want the fastest/easiest way to handle a state change, doing it once with a `classList` update will be faster.

ARIA attributes as CSS selectors

In our preferred CSS syntax, writing that change within a single set of braces would look like this:

```
.co-Button {
    background-color: $color-button-passive;
    &[aria-selected="true"] {
        background-color: $color-button-selected;
    }
}
```

We use the ampersand (&) as a parent selector and the attribute selector to leverage the enhanced specificity having the aria attribute on the node provides. Then we can just style the changes as needed.

The ability to nest state changes within a rule in this manner provides increased developer ergonomics. The intention is that a rule is only defined at root level once throughout the entire application styles. This provides a single source of truth to define all possible eventualities pertaining to that class. For more information, ensure you read Chapter 8, *The Ten Commandments of Sane Style Sheets*.

As a related note, the *CSS Selectors Level 4 specification* (https://drafts.cs swg.org/selectors-4/#attribute-case) makes provision for case insensitivity by using a i flag before the closing square bracket. For example:

```
css .co-Button { background-color: $color-button-passive;
&[aria-selected="true" i] { background-color: $color-
button-selected; } }
```

This allows any case value variant of the attribute to pass (by default it is case sensitive)

States and properties, redone with ARIA

This section of the WAI-ARIA specification describes *Widget Attributes*, these contain many of the common states needed when working with a web application and rapidly changing data.

Here are the examples given at the beginning of this chapter re-written using ARIA:

- `aria-disabled="true"` (used instead of `is-Suspended`)
- `aria-live="polite"` (used instead of `.is-Live`, the polite value is one of *three possible values* (https://www.w3.org/TR/wai-aria/states_and_properties#aria-live) to describe how updates should be communicated)
- `aria-current="true"` (this one is currently proposed for WAI-ARIA 1.1 http://www.w3.org/TR/wai-aria-1.1/#aria-current)
- `aria-busy="true"` (used instead of `is-Busy`, to indicate the element and it's subtree (if any) are busy

There are plenty more and the specification is, by W3C specification standards, easy to understand.

If ARIA can't be used

If, for whatever reason, you aren't able to use `aria-*` attributes to communicate state in a site or application. I now tend to lean towards naming selectors without using the micro-namespace to designate state. For example, instead of:

```
<button class="co-Button is-Selected">Old Skool
Button</button>
```

I would instead recommend using a variant version of the selector like this:

```
<button class="co-Button co-Button-selected">Old Skool Button</button>
```

This keeps the context of the module in tact and merely indicates a variant of this same class is being applied.

You should be aware that there is a *gotcha* when using attribute selectors to communicate state. Certain older versions of Android (Android 4.0.3 stock browser as an example) don't force a re-calculation of styles when an attribute value is changed. The upshot of this is that any styles that rely on a attribute won't work dynamically (for example when toggled with JavaScript). There are two possible workarounds. Firstly, you can toggle a class somewhere in the DOM at the same time you change the attribute. Alternatively, you can initiate the attribute selectors by listing empty rules for each somewhere in the CSS. Even chaining together works e.g. `[aria-thing][aria-thing2]{}`. Either option certainly adds an undesirable complication to proceedings. A bug report of this behaviour can be found for WebKit here: `https://bugs.webkit.org/show_bug.cgi?id=64372` and the workaround mentioned came courtesy of this Stack Overflow question: `http://stackoverflow.com/questions/6655364/css-attribute-selector-descendant-gives-a-bug-in-webkit/`

Summary

Using WAI-ARIA states to communicate changes in the DOM provides styling hooks that are as useful and easy to use as standard HTML classes. Although purely preference, I'm also a fan of the fact that an entirely different selector is used to communicate state in the style sheets; it is simpler to spot within a rule.

None of those prior factors really get you anything new. What using WAI-ARIA states will do, virtually for free, is start to provide a better means of communicating your web application state to users of assistive technology. If money talks, consider also that by using WAI-ARIA you are widening your product up to a greater number of users (see the additional info below).

As such, using WAI-ARIA states and properties, is the recommended means of communicating state in projects adopting a ECSS methodology.

Additional information and statistics from the Royal National Institute for the Blind (RNIB)

The *RNIB* (http://rnib.org.uk/) was kind enough to supply a little data regarding the number of blind people here in the UK. These may prove useful when arguing/considering a case for using ARIA states in your project:

- There are just over 84,000 registered blind and partially sighted people of working age in the UK (out of an estimated population of around 64 million).

However, according to the government's Labour Force Survey, around 185,000 people of working age in the UK have a self-reported *seeing difficulty*. This includes people whose sight loss would not be eligible for registration, but which is still of sufficient severity to affect their everyday lives. It also includes those who do not consider themselves as disabled. Of the 185,000:

- 113,000 consider themselves as long-term disabled with a *seeing difficulty*
- 72,000 consider themselves as not disabled with a *seeing difficulty*
- Estimated number of people in the UK living with sight loss in 2011 – 1,865,900
- Estimated number of people in the UK predicted to be living with sight loss in 2020 – 2,269,700
- Estimated number of adults with diabetes, a major cause of visual impairments in 2012 – 3,866,980

7
Applying ECSS to Your Website or Application

In this Chapter we are going to cover the following topics:

- Applying ECSS to logic modules
- Applying ECSS to visual modules
- Organising modules, their components and naming files
- Working with generated content from a CMS
- ECSS and global styles

ECSS is a good match for complex web applications. First up, let's consider how we might apply ECSS around the logic of a large application.

Applying ECSS to logic modules

Typically, in a web application, some programming language (e.g. JavaScript/TypeScript/Ruby/whatever), will be generating *a thing*.

It's often practical and desirable to use the file name of that thing as the name of the module (or component of a module). Therefore, if a file is called `Header.js` and generates the container for the header, any component parts of that header could be named accordingly. For example, in ECSS parlance, a company registration number might get `sw-Header_Reg` as its selector. By extension, a search box component inside the header might have a selector like `sw-HeaderSearch_Input` (the input box created by the `HeaderSearch.js` file).

An example

Let's consider a more concrete example. Suppose we are authoring a JavaScript client-side application and we have a component called ShoppingCartLines.js. Its task is to render out the lines within a shopping cart and it in turn displays within a module called ShoppingCart.js. The ShoppingCart module renders out anything to do with the shopping cart itself. Straight forward enough so far.

Now let's complicate our imagined scenario a little by suggesting that our shopping cart will work within a modal view in some scenarios and as part of the page, in normal document flow, in others.

In this instance, we have a wider module: ShoppingCart and a component that typically lives within the module called ShoppingCartLines. Each of those will have their own child nodes. The module and component have two possible views: in a modal and in the page. Let's also imagine that the switch of contexts would be handled by the application logic.

Our constant is the module itself and we can use a namespace to provide context for it. When applying ECSS around application logic it makes sense to always use the full name of the application module or component as the module section of the ECSS style selector. This has the benefit of making all HTML classes in the DOM self descriptive as to their origin and purpose.

 When naming the class for the outermost container of a module or component, no child extension should be added to the class/selector. Only the child parts of a module or component should get the node extension.

OK, so, at this point, our selectors could be named like this in the style sheets:

```
.mod-ShoppingCart {} /*Modal*/
.page-ShoppingCart {} /*Page*/
.mod-ShoppingCartLines {} /*Modal*/
.page-ShoppingCartLines {} /*Page*/
```

This way our module and component have their two contexts isolated by a namespace switch. We are free to style each as we see fit with no potential leakage of styles from one to the other. This is the exact kind of scenario that typically becomes fraught when components and modules share HTML classes in the interest of abstraction and re-use.

Let's consider a twist on this scenario. Let's suppose we don't switch contexts with application logic. Instead, we have a switch of styles with media queries. We have a modal implementation at smaller viewports and the page style, in normal document flow, at larger viewports.

In this instance, we could have a single namespace e.g. `sc-ShoppingCart` (I'm using `sc-` to designate the context is `ShoppingCart`) and use media queries in the CSS to provide visual changes.

For example:

```
.sc-ShoppingCart {
    /*Modal styles for smaller viewports*/
    @media (min-width: $M) {
        /* Page styles for larger viewports */
    }
}

.sc-ShoppingCartLines {
    /* Modal styles for smaller viewports */
    @media (min-width: $M) {
        /* Page styles for larger viewports */
    }
}
```

Child nodes of a module or component

As mentioned previously, a module or component will have its own child node elements. These selectors should be named with a child extension. For example:

```
.sc-ShoppingCart {
    /* The root of the component/module, no child
    extension needed */
}

.sc-ShoppingCart_Title {
    /* The 'title' child node of the Shopping Cart */
}

.sc-ShoppingCart_Close {
    /* A 'close' button child of the Shopping Cart for
    when the cart is modal */
}
```

Each child gets the namespace and component (or module) name of its parent.

Full details on the ECSS naming convention are in `Chapter 5`, *File Organisation and Naming Conventions*.

So, at this point we now have an understanding of how we might name our selectors when applying ECSS around application modules and logic. We will look now at how we might name selectors and apply ECSS around purely visual modules. However, first a brief but important tangent on using type selectors.

A note on type selectors

When authoring CSS, there are occasions when it can be tempting to use type selectors. Usually this is when there are HTML5 text-level elements, such as `<i>`, `<b>`, `<em>` or `<span>`. For example, suppose we have a sentence with a couple of words that need to be bold. Then temptation would be to do this:

```
<p class="ch-ShoppingCart_TextIntro">Here is the contents
of your cart. You currently have <b>5 items</b>.</p>
```

And use these selectors to apply styles to the contents of that `b` tag:

```
.ch-ShoppingCart_TextIntro {
    /* Styles for the text */
    b {
      /* Styles for the bold section within */
    }
}
```

There are a couple of problems here:

1. We have created a dependency on certain markup structure (it must be a child node and be a b tag).
2. Due to point 1, we have created a selector that is more specific than it needs to be. This makes any future overrides more difficult to reason about and perform.

While it may seem overly verbose, this is how that scenario should be handled:

```
<p class="ch-ShoppingCart_TextIntro">Here is the contents of your cart. You
currently have <b class="ch-ShoppingCart_TextIntroStrong">5 items</b>.</p>
```

And this CSS:

```
.ch-ShoppingCart_TextIntro {
    /* Styles for the text */
}

.ch-ShoppingCart_TextIntroStrong {
    /* Styles for the bold section within */
}
```

Each element has its own selector and rule. Neither depends upon the other. Neither rule requires particular markup to be applied.

Each rule applied to an element should be as opinionated about its own appearance as possible. For example, it you have an element that contains two text nodes it seems logical to apply the font size and line height to the wrapping element so the two text nodes will inherit from it. However, this prevents that text node being moved to another location and rendering consistently. Instead, apply the color, font-size and line-height to each node, even if they are initially very similar (perhaps at the outset only the colour differs). It will seem counter-intuitive at first but protects against possible deviations in the future (being moved in the DOM, styles diverging etc).

Applying ECSS to visual modules

Visual components refers to areas of markup that are not necessarily generated by a particular piece of application logic.

You can still break areas into logical **visual** areas and apply ECSS to them. This is the approach employed on the `http://ecss.io` website.

There are no hard and fast rules. As an example, we might break a design into visual areas for Structure, Menu, Footer, Navigation, Quick Jump Menu, Hero Image etc.

And in this case, our selectors look like this:

```
.st-Header {
    /* Structural container for header */
}

.st-Footer {
    /* Structural container for footer */
}
```

However, we might just as easily do this:

```
.hd-Outer {
    /* Structural container for header */
}

.ft-Outer {
    /* Structural container for footer */
}
```

Or even like this if it's the module:

```
.hd-Header {
    /* Structural container for the Header module */
}

.ft-Footer {
    /* Structural container for the footer module */
}
```

None of those approaches is wrong or right. As long as child nodes/selectors follow the same naming convention, the styles will be isolated to the particular area.

The reality is that on smaller sites, you could use pretty much any class-naming approach you like and the dangers of collision would be minimal. However, as soon as projects start to grow the benefits of namespacing and a strict naming convention will start to pay you back handsomely. Just make a decision, and apply that choice consistently.

Organising modules, their components, and naming files

At this point, I think it will be useful to consider a more detailed example module structure. It's similar to the structure in which I'm used to employing ECSS. It's a little more involved than our prior examples and gives another subtly different variation on how files could be organised and selectors named. As ever, from our CSS point of view our aim is isolation, consistency and solid developer ergonomics. Let's take a look.

Suppose we have a module. Its job is to load the sidebar area of our site. The directory structure might initially look like this:

```
SidebarModule/ => everything SidebarModule related lives in here
    /assets => any assets (images etc) for the module
    /css => all CSS files
    /min => minified CSS/JS files
    /components => all component logic for the module in
    here
    css-namespaces.json => a file to define all namespaces
    SidebarModule.js => logic for the module
    config.json => config for the module
```

In terms of the example markup structure this module should produce, we would expect something like this initially:

```
<div class="sb-SidebarModule">

</div>
```

The CSS that styles this initial element should live inside the `css` folder like this:

```
SidebarModule/
   /assets
   /css
      /components
      SidebarModule.css
/min
/components
css-namespaces.json
SidebarModule.js
config.json
```

Now, suppose we have a component inside the `SidebarModule` that creates a header for the `SidebarModule`. We might name the component with a file called `Header.js` and store it inside the components sub-folder of our `SidebarModule` like this:

```
SidebarModule/
   /assets
   /css
      /components
      SidebarModule.css
/min
/components
   Header.js
css-namespaces.json
SidebarConfig.js
SidebarModule.js
config.json
```

With that in place, the `Header.js` might render markup like this:

```
<div class="sb-SidebarModule">
    <div class="sb-Header">
        <div class="sb-Header_Logo"></div>
    </div>
</div>
```

Note how the `Header` component, due to being within the context of the `SidebarModule` carries the sb- micro-namespace to designate its parentage. And the nodes created by this new component are named according to the logic that creates them.

In terms of the general conventions to follow:

Components should carry the micro-namespace of the originating logic. If you are creating a component that sits within a module, it should carry a/the namespace of the originating module (possible namespaces for a module are defined in `css-namespaces.json`).

HTML classes/CSS selectors should be named according to the file name/components that generated them. For example, if we created another component inside our module called `HeaderLink.js` which renders its markup inside a child of the `Header.js` component, then the markup it generates and the applicable CSS selectors should match this file name.

For example:

```html
<div class="sb-SidebarModule">
    <div class="sb-HeaderPod">
        <div class="sb-HeaderPod_Logo"></div>
    </div>
    <div class="sb-HeaderPod_Nav">
        <div class="sb-HeaderLink">Node Value</div>
        <div class="sb-HeaderLink">Node Value</div>
        <div class="sb-HeaderLink">Node Value</div>
        <div class="sb-HeaderLink">Node Value</div>
    </div>
</div>
```

In terms of the folder structure, it would now look like this:

```
SidebarModule/
  /assets
  /css
    /components
       Header.css
       HeaderLink.css
    SidebarModule.css
  /min
  /components
    Header.js
    HeaderLink.js
  css-namespaces.json
  SidebarConfig.js
  SidebarModule.js
  tsconfig.json
```

Notice how there is a 1:1 correlation between component logic (the `*.js` file) and the associated styles (the `*.css` files) – both sit within a `components` sub-folder. Although both logic and styles don't share the same immediate parent folder, they both live within the same module folder, making removal of the entire module simple if needed.

Nodes within a component

To recap. Used in this way, the ECSS naming convention of nodes within a component should always be:

```
ns-Component_Node-variant
```

- `ns` : The micro-namespace (always lower-case)
- `-Component`: The Component name (always upper camel-case)
- `_Node`: The child node of a component (always upper camel-case preceded by an underscore)
- `-variant`: The optional variant of a node (always lower-case and preceded by a hyphen)

Variants

Note that the `-variant` part of a node within a component is optional and should only be used to denote subtle variations on otherwise identical items. For example, multiple headers that are identical apart from a differing background image might be rendered like this:

```
<div class="sb-Classification_Header sb-Classification_Header-2"></div>
```

Remember, we discussed the use of variant selectors a little more in Chapter 5, *File Organisation and Naming Conventions*.

Working with generated content from a CMS

It's probable that if you use ECSS with any sort of content management system (WordPress, Ghost, Drupal et al) you will encounter a situation where it's not possible to add a class to every element. For example, in a WordPress page or post, it would be unrealistic to expect users entering content to remember the right class to add to each paragraph tag. In these situations, I think pragmatism has to win out.

Set a ECSS class to the enclosing element and (grudgingly) accept that all the nested elements will be set with a type selector. Here's some example markup:

```
<main class="st-Main">
    <h1>How to survive in South Central?</h1>
    <p>A place where bustin' a cap is fundamental. </p>
    <ul>
        <li>Rule number one: get yourself a gun. A nine in yo' ass'll be
fine</li>
        <li>Rule number two: don't trust nobody.</li>
    </ul>

</main>
```

Here is how you might author the CSS to handle selecting those elements:

```
.st-Main {
    h1 {
        /* Styles for h1 */
    }
    p {
        /* Styles for p */
    }
    ul {
        /* Styles for ul */
    }
    li {
        /* Styles for li */
    }
}
```

I'm not crazy about that. We're nesting selectors, tying our styles to elements, basically everything we normally want to avoid with ECSS. However, I'm being honest. The reality is that this is likely going to be the best compromise we can manage. Where it is possible to add a class to elements we absolutely should. However, there will be situations where this simply isn't possible and no amount of Ivory Tower idealism will help in those situations. Remember *Pin Cing Do!*

ECSS and global styles

Whilst the Lion's share of CSS in a web application can be described as module based, there is an inevitable amount of global CSS we need to deal with. From an ECSS perspective we should keep this global CSS as minimal as possible. Typically, besides any requisite *reset* styles, there will be a default font-size, font-family and perhaps some default colours. These are styles that are usually applied to type selectors. Unless you have classes on the root HTML element of body for example.

 If you are looking for a base set of reset styles for a web application you may find my *App Reset* CSS useful. You can find it on GitHub here: `https ://github.com/benfrain/app-reset` or install via NPM with `npm install app-reset`.

There may also be some global structure needed. For example, if you have a common structure throughout your application (header, footer, sidebar etc), you may want to create some selectors to reflect this. In the past I have used a `.st-` or `.sw-` micro-namespace to define *Structure* or *Site Wide* but you can use whatever is most apt for you. However, my advice would be that there really shouldn't be many of these selectors as these typically relate to very broad areas that all the modules of an application should live within.

In terms of organising global CSS I currently favour a folder in the root of any project called `globalCSS`. In that folder would be any variables, mixins, global image assets, any font or icon-font files, a basic CSS reset file and any global CSS needed.

Summary

We've looked at the two principal ways you might apply ECSS in this chapter. We've also considered a possible folder structure for a complete and more complicated module. I'm hopeful that by this point, you'll have a fair idea of how you might apply ECSS in your projects.

Hand-in-hand with the architectural approach of implementing CSS is the practice of actually authoring your style sheets. You know, how the code actually looks in the editor. The code samples throughout this book have been demonstrating this syntax but it's time now to delve into it in more detail.

How to best author style sheets to put all this ECSS malarkey into practice is what we will look at in the next chapter.

8

The Ten Commandments of Sane Style Sheets

1. Thou shalt have a single source of truth for all key selectors
2. Thou shalt not nest, unless thou art nesting media queries or overrides
3. Thou shalt not use ID selectors, even if thou thinkest thou hast to
4. Thou shalt not write vendor prefixes in the authoring style sheets
5. Thou shalt use variables for sizing, colours and z-index
6. Thou shalt always write rules mobile first (avoid max-width)
7. Use mixins sparingly, and avoid @extend
8. Thou shalt comment all magic numbers and browser hacks
9. Thou shalt not inline images
10. Thou shalt not write complicated CSS when simple CSS will work just as well

Blessed are those that follow these rules for they shall inherit sane style sheets.

Amen.

Why the ten commandments?

The following, highly opinionated, set of rules came about as a way to author predictable style sheets across teams of developers. Each rule can be enforced with tooling. When there is just one CSS developer on a project, spending time developing or integrating tooling may seem superfluous. However, beyond a couple of active developers the tooling will earn its time investment time and again. We will deal with the tooling to *police* the rules in the next chapter. For now, let's consider the syntax and the rules themselves.

Tooling

To achieve more maintainable style sheets we can lean upon PostCSS, a piece of CSS tooling that allows the manipulation of CSS with JavaScript. The curious can look here for more information: `https://github.com/postcss/postcss`

PostCSS facilitates the use of an extended CSS syntax. For the purpose of authoring, the syntax used borrows heavily from *Sass* (`http://sass-lang.com/`). This provides functionality to make our authoring style sheets easier to maintain.

Using PostCSS we are able to make use of:

- Variables
- Mixins (like macros for certain settings such as font-families)
- Referencing a **key-selector** with an ampersand symbol (`&`)

Practically, PostCSS can enable similar functionality to a CSS pre-processor such as Sass, LESS or Stylus.

Where it differs is in its modularity and extensibility. Rather than *swallow the whole pill* as is needed with the aforementioned pre-processors, using PostCSS allows us to be more selective about the feature set we employ. It also allows us to easily extend our feature set at will, either with any number of *off the peg* plugins, or, by writing our own plugins with JavaScript.

For example, where Sass allows loops to be written, we choose to prevent that capability. For instance where looping is needed to solve a specific problem (for example, 100 variants of different coloured headers) we can still achieve that buy as a PostCSS plugin written in JavaScript.

In addition, thanks to the PostCSS ecosystem, we can perform static analysis of the authoring styles with linting; failing builds and code commits when undesirable code is authored.

 In case the term *linting* is alien to you, it's another term for static analysis. It looks at the authored code and makes suggestions based on any number of pre-defined rules. For example, it might issue a warning if you use floats, or don't put white-space or a semi-colon where required. Generally speaking, you can use linters to enforce any kind of coding conventions you like and while more than useful when working alone, they can be priceless when working in teams: where many (careless) hands might touch the code.

Rationale

When we are authoring ECSS, we want to avoid producing CSS that suffers from being overly specific, littered with unneeded prefixes, poorly commented and full of *magic* numbers.

The following 10 rules set-out what are considered to be the most important rules to achieve this goal.

Definitions used throughout:

- **Override**: A situation where the values of a key selector are purposely amended based upon inheritance
- **Key selector**: The right most selector in any CSS rule
- **Prefixes**: Vendor specific prefixes e.g. `-webkit-transform:`
- **Authoring style sheets**: The files we author the styling rules in
- **CSS**: The resultant CSS file generated by the tooling and ultimately consumed by the browser

Let's now consider each rule and the problem it aims to solve.

1. Thou shalt have a single source of truth for all key selectors

In the authoring style sheets, a key selector should only be written once.

This allows us to search for a key-selector in the code base and find a *single source of truth* for our selector. Thanks to the use of an extended CSS syntax, everything that happens to that key selector can be encapsulated in a single rule block.

Overrides to the key selector are handled by nesting and referencing the key selector with the *parent* selector. More of which shortly.

Consider this example:

```
.key-Selector {
    width: 100%;
    @media (min-width: $M) {
        width: 50%;
```

```
        }
    .an-Override_Selector & {
        color: $color-grey-33;
    }
}
```

That would yield the following in the CSS:

```
.key-Selector {
  width: 100%;
}

@media (min-width: 768px) {
  .key-Selector {
    width: 50%;
  }
}

.an-Override_Selector .key-Selector {
  color: #333;
}
```

In the authoring style sheets, the key selector (`.key-Selector`) is never repeated at a root level. Therefore, from a maintenance point of view, we only have to search for `.key-Selector` in the code base and we will find everything that could happen to that key selector described in a single location; a single source of truth.

- What happens if we need it to display differently in a different viewport size?
- What happens when it lives within containerX?
- What happens when this or that class gets added to it via JavaScript?

In all these instances the eventualities for that key selector are nested within that single rule block. This means that any possible specificity issues are entirely isolated within a single set of curly braces.

Let's look at overrides in further detail next.

Dealing with overrides

In the prior example, there was a demonstration of how to deal with an override to a key selector. We nest the overriding selector inside the rule block of the key selector and reference the parent with the `&` symbol. The `&` symbol, as in the Sass language, is a parent selector. It might help you to think of it as being roughly equivalent to `this` in JavaScript.

To test rules using the parent selector I recommend `http://sassmeister.com`

Standard override

Consider this example:

```
.ip-Carousel {
    font-size: $text13;
    /* The override is here for when this key-selector sits within a ip-
HomeCallouts element */
    .ip-HomeCallouts & {
        font-size: $text15;
    }
}
```

This would yield the following CSS:

```
.ip-Carousel {
  font-size: 13px;
}

.ip-HomeCallouts .ip-Carousel {
  font-size: 15px;
}
```

This results in a `font-size` increase for the `ip-Carousel` when it is inside an element with a class of `ip-HomeCallouts`.

Override with additional class on same element

Let's consider another example, what if we need to provide an override when this element gets an additional class? We should do that like this:

```
.ip-Carousel {
    background-color: $color-green;
    &.ip-ClassificationHeader {
        background-color: $color-grey-a7;
    }
}
```

That would yield this CSS:

```
.ip-Carousel {
  background-color: #14805e;
}

.ip-Carousel.ip-ClassificationHeader {
  background-color: #a7a7a7;
}
```

Again, the override is contained within the rule block for the key selector.

Override when inside another class and also has an additional class

Finally let's consider the eventuality where we need to provide an override for a key selector inside another element that also has an additional class present:

```
.ip-Carousel {
    background-color: $color-green;
    .home-Container &.ip-ClassificationHeader {
        background-color: $color-grey-a7;
    }
}
```

That would yield the following CSS:

```
.ip-Carousel {
  background-color: #14805e;
}

.home-Container .ip-Carousel.ip-ClassificationHeader {
  background-color: #a7a7a7;
}
```

We have used the parent selector here to reference our key selector between an override above (`.home-Container`) and alongside another class (`.ip-ClassificationHeader`).

Override with media queries

Finally, let's consider overrides with media queries. Consider this example:

```
.key-Selector {
    width: 100%;
    @media (min-width: $M) {
```

```
    width: 50%;
  }
}
```

That would yield this CSS:

```
.key-Selector {
  width: 100%;
}

@media (min-width: 768px) {
  .key-Selector {
    width: 50%;
  }
}
```

Again, all eventualities contained within the same rule. Note the use of a variable for the media query width? We will come to that shortly.

Any and all media queries should be contained in the same manner. Here's a more complex example:

```
.key-Selector {
    width: 100%;
    @media (min-width: $M) and (max-width: $XM) and (orientation: portrait)
{
        width: 50%;
    }
    @media (min-width: $L) {
        width: 75%;
    }
}
```

That would yield this CSS:

```
.key-Selector {
  width: 100%;
}

@media (min-width: 768px) and (max-width: 950px) and (orientation:
portrait) {
  .key-Selector {
    width: 50%;
  }
}

@media (min-width: 1200px) {
  .key-Selector {
```

```
        width: 75%;
    }
}
```

With all the nesting of overrides we have just looked at, you may think it makes sense to nest child elements too? You are wrong. Very wrong. This would be a very, very bad thing to do. We'll look at why next.

2. Thou shalt not nest, unless thou art nesting media queries or overrides

The key selector in CSS is the rightmost selector in any rule. It is the selector upon which the enclosed property/values are applied.

We want our CSS rules to be as *flat* as possible. We **DO NOT** want other selectors before a key selector (or any DOM element) unless we absolutely need them to override the default key selector styles.

The reason being that adding additional selectors and using element types (for example `h1.yes-This_Selector`):

- Creates additional unneeded specificity
- Makes it harder to maintain, as subsequent overrides need to be ever more specific
- Adds unneeded bloat to the resultant CSS file
- In the case of element types, ties the rule to a specific element and/or markup structure

For example, suppose we have a CSS rule like this:

```
#notMe .or-me [data-thing="nope"] .yes-This_Selector {
    width: 100%;
}
```

In that above example, `yes-This_Selector` is the key selector. If those property/values should be added to the key selector in all eventualities, we should make a simpler rule.

To simplify that prior example, if all we want to target is the key-selector we would want a rule like this:

```
.yes-This_Selector {
    width: 100%;
}
```

Don't nest children within a rule

Suppose we have a situation where we have a video play button inside a wrapping element. Consider this markup:

```
<div class="med-Video">
    <div class="med-Video_Play">Play</div>
</div>
```

Let's set some basic styling for the wrapper:

```
.med-Video {
    position: absolute;
    background-color: $color-black;
}
```

Now we want to position the play element within that wrapping element. You might be tempted to do this:

```
.med-Video {
  position: absolute;
  background-color: $color-black;
  /* Center the play button */
  .med-Video_Play {
      position: absolute;
      top: 50%;
      left: 50%;
      transform: translate(-50%, -50%);
  }
}
```

That would yield this CSS (vendor prefixes removed for brevity):

```
.med-Video {
  position: absolute;
  background-color: #000;
  /* Center the play button */
}

.med-Video .med-Video_Play {
  position: absolute;
  top: 50%;
  left: 50%;
  transform: translate(-50%, -50%);
}
```

Do you see the problem here? We have introduced additional specificity for our `.med-Video_Play` element when it is completely unneeded.

This is a subtle illustration. However, it is important to be aware of this, and avoid doing it, lest we end up with rules like this:

```
.MarketGrid > .PhoneOnlyContainer > .ClickToCallHeader >
.ClickToCallHeaderMessage > .MessageHolder > span {
  font-weight: bold;
  padding-right: 5px;
}
```

Instead, remember that *each key selector gets its own rule block*. Overrides are nested, child elements are not. Here is that example rewritten correctly:

```
.med-Video {
    position: absolute;
    background-color: $color-black;
}

/* Center the play button */
.med-Video_Play {
    position: absolute;
    top: 50%;
    left: 50%;
```

```
    transform: translate(-50%, -50%);
}
```

That would yield this CSS:

```
.med-Video {
  position: absolute;
  background-color: #000;
}

/* Center the play button */
.med-Video_Play {
  position: absolute;
  top: 50%;
  left: 50%;
  transform: translate(-50%, -50%);
}
```

Each key selector is only as specific as it needs to be and no more.

3. Thou shalt not use ID selectors, even if thou thinkest thou hast to

The limitations of IDs in a complex UI are well documented. In summary, they are far more specific than a class selector – therefore making overrides more difficult. Plus they can only be used once in the page anyway so their efficacy is limited.

 Remember we dealt with specificity in detail back in `Chapter 2`, *The Problems of CSS at Scale.*

With ECSS we do not use ID selectors in the CSS. They present no advantages over class based selectors and introduce unwanted problems.

In the almost unbelievable situation where you HAVE to use an ID to select an element, use it within an attribute selector instead to keep specificity lower:

```
[id="Thing"] {
    /* Property/Values Here */
}
```

4. Thou shalt not write vendor prefixes in the authoring style sheets

Thanks to PostCSS, we now have tooling that means it is unnecessary to write vendor prefixes for any W3C specified property/values in the authoring style sheets. The prefixes are handled auto-magically by the *Autoprefixer* (https://github.com/postcss/autoprefixer) tool that can be configured to provide vendor prefixes for the required level of platforms/browser support.

For example, don't do this:

```
.ip-Header_Count {
  position: absolute;
  right: $size-full;
  top: 50%;
  -webkit-transform: translateY(-50%);
  -ms-transform: translateY(-50%);
  transform: translateY(-50%);
}
```

Instead you should just write this:

```
.ip-Header_Count {
    position: absolute;
    right: $size-full;
    top: 50%;
    transform: translateY(-50%);
}
```

Not only does this make the authoring style sheets easier to read and work with, it also means that when we want to change our level of support we can make a single change to the build tool and the vendor prefixes that get added will update automatically.

The only exception to this scenario is non-W3C property/values that might still be desirable. For example, for touch inertia scrolling panels in WebKit devices, it will still be necessary to add certain vendor prefixed properties in the authoring styles as they are non-W3C. For example:

```
.ui-ScrollPanel {
    -webkit-overflow-scrolling: touch;
```

```
    }
```

Or in the case of removing the scrollbar for WebKit:

```
.ui-Component {
    &::-webkit-scrollbar {
      -webkit-appearance: none;
    }
}
```

5. Thou shalt use variables for sizing, colours and z-index

For any project of size, setting variables for sizing, colours, and z-index is essential.

UIs are typically based upon some form of grid or sizing ratio. Therefore sizing should be based upon set sizes, and sensible delineations of those sizes. For example here is 11px based sizing and variants as variables:

```
$size-full: 11px;
$size-half: 5.5px;
$size-quarter: 2.75px;
$size-double: 22px;
$size-treble: 33px;
$size-quadruple: 44px;
```

For a developer, the use of variables offers additional economies. For example, it saves colour picking values from composites. It also helps to normalise designs.

For example, if a project uses only 13px, 15px and 22px font sizes and a change comes through requesting 14px font-sizing, the variables provide some normalisation reference. In this case, should the fonts be 13px or 15px as 14px is not used anywhere else? This allows developers to feedback possible design inconsistencies to the designers.

The same is true of colour values. For example, suppose we have a variable for the hex #333. We can write that as a variable like this:

```
$color-grey-33: #333333;
```

On the surface it seems ridiculous to write the variable name when the hex value is shorter. However, again, using variables prevents unwanted variants creeping in to the code base (e.g. #323232) and helps identify *red flags* in the code.

It's also important to still use the variables when making amendments to colours. Use colour functions on the variables to achieve your goal. For example, suppose we want a semi-opaque #333 colour.

That should be achieved in the authoring style sheets like this:

```
.ip-Header {
    background-color: color($color-grey-33 a(.5));
}
```

PostCSS can provide a polyfill for the W3C colour functions: https://drafts.csswg.org/css-color/#modifying-colors and the example above yields this CSS:

```
.ip-Header {
    background-color: rgba(51, 51, 51, 0.5);
}
```

In this example we have used the alpha CSS colour function. We use the color() function, pass in the colour we want to manipulate and then the manipulation (alpha in this instance).

Using the variables can initially seem more complex but makes it easier for future authors to reason about what colour is being manipulated.

I'd also encourage you to look at *CSS Color Guard* (https://github.com/SlexAxton/css-colorguard) which is a tool to warn of colours in your codebase that are visually indistinguishable from other colours in your codebase.

The use of variables for z-index is equally important. This enforces some sanity when it comes to stacking contexts. There should be no need for z-index: 999 or similar. Instead, use one of only a few defaults (set as variables). Here are some relevant variables for z-index:

```
$zi-highest: 50;
$zi-high: 40;
$zi-medium: 30;
$zi-low: 20;
$zi-lowest: 10;
$zi-ground: 0;
$zi-below-ground: -1;
```

6. Thou shalt always write rules mobile first (avoid max-width)

For any responsive work, we want to embrace a mobile-first mentality in our styles. Therefore, the properties and values within the root of a rule should be the properties that apply to the smallest viewports (e.g. mobile). We then use media queries to override or add to these styles as and when needed.

Consider this:

```
.med-Video {
    position: relative;
    background-color: $color-black;
    font-size: $text13;
    line-height: $text15;
    /* At medium sizes we want to bump the text up */
    @media (min-width: $M) {
        font-size: $text15;
        line-height: $text18;
    }
    /* Text and line height changes again at larger
    viewports */
    @media (min-width: $L) {
        font-size: $text18;
        line-height: 1;
    }
}
```

That would yield this CSS:

```
.med-Video {
  position: relative;
  background-color: #000;
  font-size: 13px;
  line-height: 15px;
}

@media (min-width: 768px) {
  .med-Video {
    font-size: 15px;
    line-height: 18px;
  }
}

@media (min-width: 1200px) {
  .med-Video {
```

```
      font-size: 18px;
      line-height: 1;
   }
 }
```

We only need to change the `font-size` and `line-height` at different viewports so that is all we are amending. By using `min-width` (and not `max-width`) in our media query, should the `font-size` and `line-height` need to stay the same at a larger size viewport we wouldn't need any extra media queries. We only need a media query when things change going up the viewport size range. To this ends, the use of `max-width` as the single argument of a media query is discouraged.

Bottom line: write media queries with `min-width` not `max-width`. The only exception here is if you want to isolate some style to a middle range. For example between medium and large viewports. Example:

```
.med-Video {
    position: relative;
    background-color: $color-black;
    font-size: $text13;
    line-height: $text15;
    /* Between medium and large sizes we want to bump the
    text up */
    @media (min-width: $M) and (max-width: $L) {
        font-size: $text15;
        line-height: $text18;
    }
}
```

7. Use mixins sparingly (and avoid @extend)

Avoid the temptation of abstracting code into mixins. There are a few areas where mixins are perfect. The code for CSS text truncation (e.g. `@mixin Truncate`) or iOS style inertia scrolling panels, where there are number of pseudo selectors to get right for different browsers. Another good use case can be complex font stacks.

Font stacks are difficult to get right and tedious to author. The sanest way I've found to deal with fonts is to have the `body` use the most common font stack and then only override this with a different font-stack as and when needed.

For example:

```scss
.med-Video {
    position: relative;
    background-color: $color-black;
    font-size: $text13;
    line-height: $text15;
    /* At medium sizes we want to bump the text up */
    @media (min-width: $M) {
        @mixin FontHeadline;
        font-size: $text15;
        line-height: $text18;
    }
}
```

For simpler font-stacks, a variable can handle this need easily so may be preferable. However, mixins are great for more complex font stacks, where it's preferable to have certain font stacks apply in certain situations. For example, perhaps one font is required for LoDPI, and another for HiDPI. These situations can't be dealt with by using a variable alone so a mixin is used as needed.

Ultimately, aim for ten or less mixins in a project. Any more than that and it's probable mixins are being abused to needlessly abstract code.

Avoid @extends

I first came across `@extend` when using Sass (`http://sass-lang.com/documentation/fil e.SASS_REFERENCE.html#extend`). The `@extend` directive makes one selector inherit the styles of another selector. While this can offer some file size benefits it can make debugging more difficult as rules are combined together in a manner that is not always possible to predict at the point of authoring.

To determine whether using `@extend` was worthwhile I did a short experiment on a Sass codebase I was working with at the time. There were 73 instances that would require a Headline font stack and 37 instances that would require a headline condensed font stack (so if going the mixin route, that's 73 `@include Headline` and 37 instances of `@include HeadlineCondensed`).

Let's look at what the file size was with no font references at all, the font references defined as mixins/@includes and then the font references as @extends

With no font references

With no font declarations at all:

105.5 KB (minified), 14.2 KB (Gzipped)

This is our *base* or control if you will. Let's look at the difference adding all our fonts in via mixins/@includes creates.

Using @includes

Using mixins (@includes in Sass) for the *Headline* and *Headline Condensed* the file size of the resultant CSS was:

146.9 KB (minified), 15.4 KB (Gzipped)

So, 1.2 KB added. How does `@extend` fare?

Using @extend

By using an `@extend` rather than an `@include`:

106.9 KB (minified), 14.5 (Gzipped); only a .3 KB file size increase.

What to conclude from this anecdotal data? For me, all other things being equal, if you absolutely want the smallest file size, perhaps `@extend` is the way to go. There is some saving, albeit minor.

However, being pragmatic, if there is any maintainability gain for you using `@include` instead of `@extend` I certainly wouldn't worry about the file size.

Personally, I don't allow `@extend` functionality in projects. It adds an additional layer of complexity to debugging for very little benefit.

8. Thou shalt comment all magic numbers and browser hacks

A variables file should exist in each project that contains all variables relevant to the project.

PostCSS facilitates variables and mixins defined in either CSS files or as JavaScript objects. You can read *more about the latter here* (https://benfrai n.com/creating-and-referencing-javascript-mixins-and-variables -with-postcss/).

If a situation arises where a pixel based value needs entering into the authoring style sheets, that isn't already defined in the variables this should serve as a red flag to you. This scenario is also covered above. In the case where a *magic* number needs entering in the authoring style sheets, ensure a comment is added on the line above to explain its relevance. This may seem superfluous at the time but think of others and yourself in 3 months time. Why did you add a negative margin of 17 pixels to that element?

Example:

```
.med-Video {
    position: relative;
    background-color: $color-black;
    font-size: $text13;
    line-height: $text15;
    /*We need some space above to accommodate the
    absolutely positioned icon*/
    margin-top: 20px;
}
```

The same goes for any device/browser hacks. You may have your own syntax but I use a comment above the start of the hack code with the prefix /*HHHack:*/ when I have to add code purely to satisfy a particular situation. Consider this:

```
.med-Video {
    background-color: $color-black;
    font-size: $text13;
    line-height: $text15;
    /*HHHack needed to force Windows Phone 8.1 to render the full width,
reference ticket SMP-234 */
    width: 100%;
}
```

These kinds of overrides should be bottom-most in the rule if at all possible. However, make sure you add a comment. Otherwise, future authors may look at your code and presume the line(s) are superfluous and remove them.

If you find you have a lot of code, purely to service a particular browser, you might consider extracting those rules (manually or with tooling) into a separate file that only gets served as needed.

9. Thou shalt not place inline images in the authoring style sheets

While we continue to support HTTP based users (as opposed to HTTP2) the practice of inlining assets provides some advantages; primarily it reduces the number of HTTP requests required to serve the page to the user. However, placing inline assets in the authoring style sheets is discouraged.

Consider this:

```
.rr-Outfit {
    min-height: $size-quadruple;
    background-image:
url(data:image/gif;base64,iVBORw0KGgoAAAANSUhEUgAAABAAAAAQCAMAAAoLQ9TAAAAA
3NCSVQICAjb4U/gAAAAw1BMVEX///8AAACEhIQAAABYWFgAAAAAAAAAAB6enomJiYAAAAiIiJ4
eHgAAABiYmJgYGAAAACJiYkAAAC0tLR/f3/IyMjHx8e/v7+vr6+fn5+ZmZmUlJSBgYFmZmYiIiI
QEBAAAAD////w8PDv7+/i4uLh4eHf39/W1tbS0tLR0dHMzMzHx8fFxcXCwsK/v7+4uLi0tLSvr6
+rq6ulpaWfn5+ZmZmQkJCPj498fHxwcHBgYGBAQEAwMDAgICAfHx8QEBAAAAAphWZmAAAAQXRST
lMAESIiMzNEVWZmZneIiKqqu8zM3d3u7u7u7u7u7u7u7u7//////////////////////////////
////////////wP/q/8AAAAJcEhZcwAACxIAAAsSAdLdfvwAAAAVdEVYdENyZWF0aW9uIFRpbWU
AMjEvNS8xMpVX8IQAAAAcdEVYdFNvZnR3YXJlAEFkb2JlIEZpcmV3b3JrcyBDUzUVxteM2AAAAw0
lEQVQYlU2P6VLCUAyFD1KvWFQ2F1ChnLLW2oIs1ZZC8/5PRW4rM+RH5uSbLCeARt2YO2Pq+I+aa
fUjRs+PplbVzfeQcbyZzoZuSZoBdyKSkQxdOx+SuQKZK/m8BZ7Iia3lT8m6BQy4/NodpYjpb9Oi
C3i/U+1NfE08iAdIamXACGgwwzq7BCGgfrIxt8pOsDbjpRu/k+Q/DBWf3auSVq/1Rz55074d16gT
0i8pq4JTPOC9MRIqEbzeXfx860eS71yj1GWENHluGjvJwAAAAElFTkSuQmCC);
}
```

How is a future author supposed to reason about what that asset is?

 If you encounter an existing inline image in style sheets, to determine what the image is you can copy and paste the data into the browser address bar.

Instead, let the tooling inline the image for you. This means the authoring style sheets can provide a clue as to what the image might be but also enables that image to be more easily swapped out. If employing the *postcss-assets* (https://github.com/assetsjs/postcss-assets) plugin, you can inline images with the inline command. Here's that prior example rewritten:

```
.rr-Outfit {
    min-height: $size-quadruple;
    background-image: inline("/path/to-image/relevant-image-name.png");
}
```

Not only is that easier to read, it also specifies the location of the existing asset. A better approach in every way.

10. Thou shalt not write complicated CSS when simple CSS will work just as well

Try and write CSS code that is as simple as possible for others to reason about in future. Loops, mixins and functions should seldom be written. As a general rule, if there are less than 10 variations of a rule, write it *by-hand*. If on the other hand you need to create background positions for a sprite sheet of 30 images, this is something that tooling should be used for.

This pursuit of simplicity should be extended in the manner layouts are achieved. If a better supported layout mechanism achieves the same goal with the same amount of DOM nodes as a less well supported one, use the former. However, if a different layout mechanism reduces the number of DOM nodes needed or presents additional benefits yet is simply unfamiliar (for example Flexbox), take the time to understand the benefits it might offer.

Summary

Rules are nothing without enforcement. When many hands are touching the CSS codebase, no amount of education, strong words or documentation can prevent the quality of your codebase getting diluted. Offering *carrots* will only get you so far, it's usually necessary to use a little *stick* too!

In this case, the *stick* will take the form of static analysis *linting* tools that can check and enforce code as authors write. This approach can prevent non-con-formant code ever making it further than the offending developers local machine. In the next chapter we will look at how to approach that, alongside tooling in general.

Here come the *Fun Police*!

Tooling for an ECSS Approach

9

In this final chapter we will look at some of the free and open-source tooling that's available to facilitate writing sane and maintainable style sheets.

When authoring the CSS for an enduring project, the technology employed to produce the CSS should be largely immaterial. We should always be aware that a better or more efficient tool may become available to achieve our aims and when possible, and if preferable, it should be embraced.

Therefore, it shouldn't matter whether Sass, PostCSS, LESS, Stylus, Myth or any other CSS processor is employed to author the style sheets. The authored style sheets should be as easy to migrate to another meta-language as possible, if and when needed.

Furthermore, the CSS processor employed should best serve the needs of the project as a whole and not merely the preferences of any individual author. That said, there are some necessary capabilities for the CSS processor so we will cover that briefly next.

CSS requisites for CSS processors

I consider a CSS processor for style sheet authoring essential. This allows a differentiation between *authoring* style sheets (the style sheets that the author writes in their CSS processor of choice) and the *resultant* CSS (the compiled and minified CSS that gets served to the user).

Despite stating that a CSS processor is essential, the requisite features needed are fairly trivial:

- **Variables**: To mitigate human errors with colour picking and specifying constants like grid measures
- **Partials**: To facilitate one-to-one parity of authoring style sheets with a feature branch, template or logic file
- **Colour manipulations**: To allow consistent manipulation of the aforementioned variables e.g. being able to adjust or easily adjust the alpha of a colour
- All other abilities are considered non-essential and should be appraised particular to the needs of the project

Building CSS from authoring style sheets

A build system of some sort is required to compile the authoring style sheets into plain CSS.

There are many tools available to perform this task e.g Grunt, Gulp, and Brocolli to name just a few. However, just as there is no universally *right* CSS processor, or CSS methodology, so there is no universally *right* build tool.

Besides merely compiling authoring style sheets into CSS, good tooling can provide further benefits.

- **Linting**: To enable code conformity and prevent non-working code reaching deployment
- **Aggressive minification**: Rebasing z-indexes, converting length values to smaller length values e.g. (while *1pt* is equivalent to *16px* it is one less character), merging alike selectors
- **Autoprefixer**: To enable fast and accurate vendor prefixing and prevent vendor prefixes being present in the authoring style sheets

For considerations of what is deemed essential, syntax-wise, in style sheet authoring, refer to `Chapter 8`, *The Ten Commandments of Sane Style Sheets*.

Save to compile, the journey of an ECSS style sheet

In terms of tooling, at the time of writing, I currently write ECSS with the help of Gulp and PostCSS plus its many and varied plugins. It's a process that has worked well so I'll document it briefly here.

 For the very curious, a little more on my *journey from Sass to PostCSS can be found here* (https://benfrain.com/breaking-up-with-sass-postcss/).

The style sheet authors write into a partial CSS file (with a *.css file extension), using a syntax that is very similar to Sass.

On saving an authoring style sheet, the Gulp watch task notices the file change and first runs the linting task. Then, providing all is well, it compiles the partial authoring style sheets to a CSS file, then auto-prefixes that CSS file and finally BrowserSync injects the changed CSS directly into the webpage I'm working on. Typically, a source map file is also created as some authors find working with source maps in the developer tools easier for debugging. All this happens before I can *Alt + Tab* into my browser window or even move my gaze from text editor to browser window.

Here's an example gulpfile.js that demonstrate how PostCSS might be setup in a Gulp based build tool:

```
//PostCSS related
var postcss = require("gulp-postcss");
var postcssImport = require("postcss-import");
var autoprefixer = require("autoprefixer");
var simpleVars = require("postcss-simple-vars");
var mixins = require("postcss-mixins");
var cssnano = require("cssnano");
var reporter = require("postcss-reporter");
var stylelint = require("stylelint");
var stylelinterConfig = require("./stylelintConfig.js");
var colorFunction = require("postcss-color-function");
var nested = require("postcss-nested");
var sourcemaps = require("gulp-sourcemaps");

// Create the styles
gulp.task("styles", ["lint-styles"], function () {

    var processors = [
```

```
        postcssImport({glob: true}),
        mixins,
        simpleVars,
        colorFunction(),
        nested,
        autoprefixer({ browsers: ["last 2 version", "safari 5", "opera
12.1", "ios 6", "android 2.3"] }),
        cssnano
    ];

    return gulp.src("preCSS/styles.css")

    // start Sourcemaps
    .pipe(sourcemaps.init())

    // We always want PostCSS to run
    .pipe(postcss(processors).on( class="st">"error", gutil.log))

    // Write a source map into the CSS at this point
    .pipe(sourcemaps.write())

    // Set the destination for the CSS file
    .pipe(gulp.dest("./build"))

    // If in DEV environment, notify user that styles have been compiled
    .pipe(notify("Yo Mofo, check dem styles!!!"))

    // If in DEV environment, reload the browser
    .pipe(reload({stream: true}));
});
```

With Gulp the build choices are fairly limitless, this is merely an illustration. However, note how the the first thing the `styles` task does, is run the `lint-styles` task.

As mentioned in previous chapters, the linting of style sheets is a very important step on a project where multiple style sheets authors are involved. Let's look a little more at that next.

Stylelint

Stylelint is a node based linting tool for the static analysis of style sheets. In layman's terms it will analyse your style sheets for the things you specifically care about and warn you of any problems.

If you use Sass you should check out *scss-lint* (`https://github.com/brig ade/scss-lint`) which provides similar functionality for Sass files.

The linting job fails the build if any authoring errors are found. Typically it's most beneficial to have linting running in two places. In the text editor (e.g. Sublime) and in the build tool (e.g. Gulp). This way, if an author has the requisite text editor then the *editor based linting* (`ht tps://github.com/kungfusheep/SublimeLinter-contrib-stylelint`) indicates problems before an author even clicks *save*.

Even if a user doesn't have in-editor linting available, the linting job runs via Gulp on save. The build step prevents compiled code making its way to production (as continuous integration software would also fail the build).

This is a massive time saver and has proved invaluable when it comes to peer-reviewing code and performing quality assurance tests.

Here is an example `.stylelintrc` configuration for Stylelint (this is for v5 of Stylelint so future/previous versions may vary slightly):

```
{
    "rules": {
        "color-hex-case": "lower",
        "color-hex-length": "long",
        "color-named": "never",
        "color-no-invalid-hex": true,
        "font-family-name-quotes": "always-where-
        required",
        "font-weight-notation": "numeric",
        "function-comma-newline-before": "never-multi-
        line",
        "function-comma-newline-after": "never-multi-
        line",
        "function-comma-space-after": "always",
        "function-comma-space-before": "never",
        "function-linear-gradient-no-nonstandard-
        direction": true,
        "function-max-empty-lines": 0,
        "function-name-case": "lower",
        "function-parentheses-space-inside": "never",
        "function-url-data-uris": "never",
        "function-url-quotes": "always",
        "function-whitespace-after": "always",
        "number-leading-zero": "never",
        "number-no-trailing-zeros": true,
```

```
"string-no-newline": true,
"string-quotes": "double",
"length-zero-no-unit": true,
"unit-case": "lower",
"unit-no-unknown": true,
"value-keyword-case": "lower",
"value-no-vendor-prefix": true,
"value-list-comma-space-after": "always",
"value-list-comma-space-before": "never",
"shorthand-property-no-redundant-values": true,
"property-case": "lower",
"property-no-unknown": true,
"property-no-vendor-prefix": true,
"declaration-bang-space-before": "always",
"declaration-bang-space-after": "never",
"declaration-colon-space-after": "always",
"declaration-colon-space-before": "never",
"declaration-empty-line-before": "never",
"declaration-block-no-duplicate-properties": true,
"declaration-block-no-ignored-properties": true,
"declaration-block-no-shorthand-property-
overrides": true,
"declaration-block-semicolon-newline-after":
"always",
"declaration-block-semicolon-newline-before":
"never-multi-line",
"declaration-block-single-line-max-declarations":
1,
"declaration-block-trailing-semicolon": "always",
"block-closing-brace-empty-line-before": "never",
"block-no-empty": true,
"block-no-single-line": true,
"block-opening-brace-newline-after": "always",
"block-opening-brace-space-before": "always",
"selector-attribute-brackets-space-inside":
"never",
"selector-attribute-operator-space-after":
"never",
"selector-attribute-operator-space-before":
"never",
"selector-attribute-quotes": "always",
"selector-class-pattern": ["^[a-z]([a-z0-9]){1,3}-[A-Z][a-zA-
Z0-9]+(_[A-Z][a-zA-Z0-9]+)?(-([a-z0-9-]+)?[a-z0-9])?$", {
"resolveNestedSelectors": true }],
"selector-combinator-space-after": "always",
"selector-combinator-space-before": "always",
"selector-max-compound-selectors": 3,
"selector-max-specificity": "0,3,0",
```

```
        "selector-no-id": true,
        "selector-no-qualifying-type": true,
        "selector-no-type": true,
        "selector-no-universal": true,
        "selector-no-vendor-prefix": true,
        "selector-pseudo-class-case": "lower",
        "selector-pseudo-class-no-unknown": true,
        "selector-pseudo-class-parentheses-space-inside":
        "never",
        "selector-pseudo-element-case": "lower",
        "selector-pseudo-element-colon-notation":
        "single",
        "selector-pseudo-element-no-unknown": true,
        "selector-max-empty-lines": 0,
        "selector-list-comma-newline-after": "always",
        "selector-list-comma-newline-before": "never-
        multi-line",
        "selector-list-comma-space-before": "never",
        "rule-nested-empty-line-before": "never",
        "media-feature-colon-space-after": "always",
        "media-feature-colon-space-before": "never",
        "media-feature-name-case": "lower",
        "media-feature-name-no-vendor-prefix": true,
        "media-feature-no-missing-punctuation": true,
        "media-feature-parentheses-space-inside": "never",
        "media-feature-range-operator-space-after":
        "always",
        "media-feature-range-operator-space-before": "always",
        "at-rule-no-unknown": [true, {"ignoreAtRules": ["mixin"]}],
        "at-rule-no-vendor-prefix": true,
        "at-rule-semicolon-newline-after": "always",
        "at-rule-name-space-after": "always",
        "stylelint-disable-reason": "always-before",
        "comment-no-empty": true,
        "indentation": 4,
        "max-empty-lines": 1,
        "no-duplicate-selectors": true,
        "no-empty-source": true,
        "no-eol-whitespace": true,
        "no-extra-semicolons": true,
        "no-indistinguishable-colors": [true, {
            "threshold": 1,
            "whitelist": [ [ "#333333", "#303030" ] ]
        }],
        "no-invalid-double-slash-comments": true
    }
}
```

This is just an example, you can set whichever rules you care about from the *ever expanding list* (http://stylelint.io/user-guide/rules/). If using these sort of tools for the first time, you might also find it useful to download/clone *ecss-postcss-shell* (https://github.co m/benfrain/ecss-postcss-shell). It's a basic Gulp setup to run the authored style sheets through PostCSS and lints the styles with Stylelint.

 I've even contributed a little code to the Stylelint project, helping to add a rule called `selector-max-specificity` for controlling the maximum level of selector specificity any selector can have. If you are involved with controlling a CSS codebase, it's a great project to get involved in.

If that wasn't enough, Stylelint is extensible. It's easy to add additional functionality. For current builds ECSS projects in my workplace we have additional Stylelint rules to:

- Ensure only overrides and media queries can be nested (prevents nests that don't use a parent (`&`) selector)
- Ensure that key selectors match ECSS naming conventions (Stylelint now has a `selector-class-pattern` rule to help with this)
- Prevent key selectors from being compound (e.g. `.ip-Selector.ip-Selector2 {}`)
- Ensure key selectors are singular (e.g. `.ip-Thing not .a-Parent .ip-Thing {}`)

These offer bespoke quality assurance that would be time consuming and error prone to perform *by hand*.

In case I'm not making it clear I want you to know that I love Stylelint and think linting is an indispensable piece of tooling for large CSS projects with multiple authors. I simply cannot recommend it highly enough.

 There's a little more about Stylelint in *this blog post* (https://benfrain.co m/floss-your-style-sheets-with-stylelint/) or via the official *Stylelint* (http://stylelint.io/) website.

Optimisation

When CSS is heading for production, it takes an extra step through *cssnano* (`http://cssnan o.co/`). It's a fantastic and modular CSS minifier by the extraordinarily talented Ben Briggs. Highly recommended.

Besides the more obvious minification step that cssnano provides, there are a number of micro-optimisations you can perform on your CSS just by incorporating plugins from the PostCSS eco-system. For example, by consistently ordering your CSS declarations, Gzip can compress the style sheet more effectively. That's not a job I want to do manually but the *postcss-sorting* (`https://github.com/hudochenkov/postcss-sorting`) plugin can do it for free. Here's comparison of Gzip file sizes using the various declaration sorting configurations.

To exemplify, I took a large test CSS file, and unsorted once Gzipped it was 37.59 kB. Here are the file sizes of that same file when Gzipped after using the other declaration sorting configurations:

- postcss-sorting: 37.54
- CSSComb: 37.46
- Yandex: 37.48
- Zen: 37.41

So at best we gain a saving of just under 1% of the original size. A tiny economy but one you can effectively get for free.

There are other such economies such as grouping alike media queries but I'll leave these micro-optimisations for you to explore should they pique your interest.

Summary

In this chapter we've covered tooling to facilitate constant code quality and an improved style sheet authoring experience. However, you should be aware that out of everything we have covered, the specific tools listed here are likely to be the most short-lived. Tooling technology moves at a blistering pace. In just three years I went from vanilla CSS, to Sass (with *scss-lint* (`https://github.com/brigade/scss-lint`)), to PostCSS and Stylelint while also moving from GUI build tools like CodeKit to JavaScript build tools Grunt, then Gulp and now NPM scripts.

I have no idea what the best choice will be in 6 months time so the take away is to think about how tooling and approaches can improve the style sheet authoring experience across your teams, not necessarily what the current tools are.

> *Be monogamous in your personal relationships and a philandering whore in your choice of tools and techniques*
> *-The Way Of Pragmatic Coding* (https://benfrain.com/be-better-front-end-developer-way-of-pragmatic-coding/)

The closing curly brace

Now my friends we have reached the end of this little book.

While I'd hope that some of you might be able to take ECSS *off the peg* and start implementing it wholesale, I'll be just as happy if it merely provokes your own journey of discovery.

At the outset I was trying to find an approach to scaling CSS that dealt with the following problems:

- To allow the easy maintenance of a large CSS codebase over time
- To allow portions of CSS code to be removed from the codebase without effecting the remaining styles
- It should be possible to rapidly iterate on any new designs
- Changing the properties and values applied to one visual element should not unintentionally effect others
- Any solution should require minimal tooling and workflow changes to implement
- Where possible, W3C standards such as ARIA should be used to communicate state change within the user interface

ECSS answers all of those problems:

- Compartmentalizing CSS into modules allows easy removal of deprecated features
- The unique naming convention avoids global naming collisions, reduces specificity and prevents unwanted changes to unrelated elements
- As all new modules are *greenfield* it's simple to build out new designs
- Despite some tooling to accommodate globbing imports and linting, we are still writing CSS in CSS files, making on-boarding developers a far easier process
- We can also embrace ARIA as a means to control and communicate state change, not just for assistive technology but in a wider sense too

The considerations of scaling CSS are a somewhat niche pursuit. In time, we will have things like *CSS Scoping* (http://www.w3.org/TR/css-scoping-1/#scope-atrule) but until then we must use the tools and techniques at our disposal to bend existing technology to our will.

I've mentioned it numerous times but there are many ways to skin this cat. Other methods may be preferable. What follows is a list of people and resources, in no particular order that may help in your own odyssey.

Until next time dear reader, I wish you the most fruitful of adventures.

> *Absorb what is useful, reject what is useless, add what is specifically your own.*
> *-Bruce Lee*

Resources

Here are some folks that often talk or write about CSS architecture/scaling:

- Thierry Koblentz: http://cssmojo.com/
- Nicolas Gallagher: http://nicolasgallagher.com/
- Kaelig Deloumeau-Prigent: http://kaelig.fr/
- Nicole Sullivan: http://www.stubbornella.org/content/
- Harry Roberts: http://csswizardry.com/
- Jonathan Snook: https://snook.ca/
- Micah Godbolt: http://www.godbolt.me/

For a discussion about using inline-styles via JavaScript: *Shop Talk show #180* (`http://shopt alkshow.com/episodes/180-panel-on-inline-styles/`)

Interesting approaches/projects around CSS:

- Radium for React: `https://github.com/FormidableLabs/radium`
- React Native for Web: `https://github.com/necolas/react-native-web`
- CSS Modules: `https://github.com/css-modules`
- Atomic CSS: `http://acss.io/`

Appendix 1

CSS Selector Performance

Back at the beginning of 2014 I was having a *debate* (I used air-quotes there people) with some fellow developers about the irrelevance, or not, of worrying about CSS selector speed.

Whenever exchanging theories/evidence about the relative speed of CSS selectors, developers often reference *Steve Souders* (`http://stevesouders.com/`) work on CSS selectors from 2009. It's used to validate claims such as *attribute selectors are slow* or *pseudo selectors are slow*.

For the last few years, I've felt these kinds of things just weren't worth worrying about. The sound-bite I have been wheeling out for years is:

> *With CSS, architecture is outside the braces; performance is inside*

But besides referencing *Nicole Sullivan's later post on Performance Calendar* (`http://calendar .perfplanet.com/2011/css-selector-performance-has-changed-for-the-better/`) to back up my conviction that the selectors used don't really matter, I had never actually tested the theory.

To try and address this, I attempted to produce some tests of my own that would settle the argument. At the least, I believed it would prompt someone with more knowledge/evidence to provide further data.

Testing selector speed

Steve Souders' aforementioned tests use JavaScript's `new Date()`. However, nowadays, modern browsers (iOS/Safari were a notable exception at the time of testing) support the *Navigation Timing API* (`https://www.w3.org/TR/navigation-timing/`) which gives us a more accurate measure we can use. For the tests, I implemented it like this:

```
<script>
    ;(function TimeThisMother() {
        window.onload = function(){
            setTimeout(function(){
            var t = performance.timing;
                alert("Speed of selection is: " + (t.loadEventEnd -
t.responseEnd) + " milliseconds");
            }, 0);
        };
    })();
</script>
```

This lets us limit the timing of the tests between the point all assets have been received (`responseEnd`) and the point the page is rendered (`loadEventEnd`).

So, I set up a very simple test. 20 different pages, all with an identical, enormous DOM, made up of 1000 identical chunks of this markup:

```
<div class="tagDiv wrap1">
  <div class="tagDiv layer1" data-div="layer1">
    <div class="tagDiv layer2">
      <ul class="tagUl">
        <li class="tagLi"><b class="tagB"><a href="/" class="tagA link"
data-select="link">Select</a></b></li>
      </ul>
    </div>
  </div>
</div>
```

20 different CSS selection methods were tested to colour the inner most nodes red. Each page differed only in the rule applied to select the inner most node within the blocks. Here were the different selectors tested and a link to the the test page for that selector:

1. Data attribute: `https://benfrain.com/selector-test/01.html`
2. Data attribute (qualified): `https://benfrain.com/selector-test/02.html`
3. Data attribute (unqualified but with value): `https://benfrain.com/selector-test/03.html`
4. Data attribute (qualified with value): `https://benfrain.com/selector-test/04.html`
5. Multiple data attributes (qualified with values): `https://benfrain.com/selector-test/05.html`
6. Solo pseudo selector (e.g. `:after`): `https://benfrain.com/selector-test/06.html`
7. Combined classes (e.g. `class1.class2`): `https://benfrain.com/selector-test/07.html`
8. Multiple classes: `https://benfrain.com/selector-test/08.html`
9. Multiple classes with child selector: `https://benfrain.com/selector-test/09.html`
10. Partial attribute matching (e.g. `[class^=`"wrap"]`): `https://benfrain.com/selector-test/10.html`
11. nth-child selector: `https://benfrain.com/selector-test/11.html`
12. nth-child selector followed by another nth-child selector: `https://benfrain.com/selector-test/12.html`
13. Insanity selection (all selections qualified, every class used e.g. `div.wrapper > div.tagDiv > div.tagDiv.layer2 > ul.tagUL > li.tagLi > b.tagB > a.TagA.link`): `https://benfrain.com/selector-test/13.html`
14. Slight insanity selection (e.g. `.tagLi .tagB a.TagA.link`): `https://benfrain.com/selector-test/14.html`
15. Universal selector: `https://benfrain.com/selector-test/15.html`
16. Element single: `https://benfrain.com/selector-test/16.html`
17. Element double: `https://benfrain.com/selector-test/17.html`
18. Element treble: `https://benfrain.com/selector-test/18.html`
19. Element treble with pseudo: `https://benfrain.com/selector-test/19.html`
20. Single class: `https://benfrain.com/selector-test/20.html`

The test was run 5 times on each browser and the result averaged across the 5 results. The browsers tested:

- Chrome 34.0.1838.2 dev
- Firefox 29.0a2 Aurora
- Opera 19.0.1326.63
- Internet Explorer 9.0.8112.16421
- Android 4.2 (7″ tablet)

A previous version of Internet Explorer (rather than the latest Internet Explorer available to me) was used to shed some light on how a *non evergreen* browser performed. All the other browsers tested received regular updates so I wanted to be sure that there wasn't a considerable difference in the way modern regularly updating browsers deal with CSS selectors and how slightly older ones do.

Want to try the same tests out for yourself? Go and grab the files from this GitHub link: `https://github.com/benfrain/css-performance-tests`. Just open each page in your browser of choice (remember the browser must support the Network Timing API to alert a response). Also be aware that when I performed the test I discarded the first couple of results as they tended to be unusually high in some browsers.

When considering the results, don't consider one browser against another. That is not the purpose of the tests. The purpose is purely to try and evaluate the comparative difference in selection speed between the different selectors employed on each browser. For example, is selector 3 any faster than selector 7 on any browser? Therefore, when looking at the table, it makes more sense to look down the columns than across the rows.

Here are the results. All times in milliseconds:

Test	Chrome 34	Firefox 29	Opera 19	IE 19	Android 4
1	56.8	125.4	63.6	152.6	1455.2
2	55.4	128.4	61.4	141	1404.6
3	55	125.6	61.8	152.4	1363.4
4	54.8	129	63.2	147.4	1421.2
5	55.4	124.4	63.2	147.4	1411.2
6	60.6	138	58.4	162	1500.4

7	51.2	126.6	56.8	147.8	1453.8
8	48.8	127.4	56.2	150.2	1398.8
9	48.8	127.4	55.8	154.6	1348.4
10	52.2	129.4	58	172	1420.2
11	49	127.4	56.6	148.4	1352
12	50.6	127.2	58.4	146.2	1377.6
13	64.6	129.2	72.4	152.8	1461.2
14	50.2	129.8	54.8	154.6	1381.2
15	50	126.2	56.8	154.8	1351.6
16	49.2	127.6	56	149.2	1379.2
17	50.4	132.4	55	157.6	1386
18	49.2	128.8	58.6	154.2	1380.6
19	48.6	132.4	54.8	148.4	1349.6
20	50.4	128	55	149.8	1393.8
Biggest Diff.	16	13.6	17.6	31	152
Lowest	13	6	13	10	6

The difference between fastest and slowest selector

The **Biggest Diff.** row shows the difference in milliseconds between the fastest and slowest selector. Of the desktop browsers, IE9 stands out as having the biggest difference between fastest and slowest selectors at **31** ms. The others are all around half of that figure. However, interestingly there .

The slowest selector

I was interested to note that the slowest selector type differed from browser to browser. Both Opera and Chrome found the *insanity* selector (test 13) the hardest to match (the similarity between Opera and Chrome here perhaps not surprising given they share the *blink* (`http://www.chromium.org/blink`) engine), while Firefox struggled with a single pseudo selector (*test 6* (`https://benfrain.com/selector-test/06.html`)), as did the Android 4.2 device (a Tesco hudl 7" tablet). Internet Explorer 9's Achilles heel was the partial attribute selector (*test 10* (`https://benfrain.com/selector-test/10.html`)).

Good CSS architecture practices

One thing we can be clear on is that using a flat hierarchy of class-based selectors, as is the case with ECSS, provides selectors that are as fast as any others.

What does this mean?

For me, it has confirmed my believe that it is absolute folly to worry about the type of selector used. Second guessing a selector engine is pointless as the manner selector engines work through selectors clearly differs. Further more, the difference between fastest and slowest selectors isn't massive, even on a ludicrous DOM size like this. As we say in the North of England, *There are bigger fish to fry*.

Since documenting my original results, Benjamin Poulain, a WebKit Engineer got in touch to point out his concerns with the methodology used. His comments were very interesting and some of the information he related is quoted verbatim below:

> By choosing to measure performance through the loading, you are measuring plenty of much much bigger things than CSS, CSS Performance is only a small part of loading a page.

If I take the time profile of `[class^="wrap"]` for example (taken on an old WebKit so that it is somewhat similar to Chrome), I see:

- ~10% of the time is spent in the rasterizer.
- ~21% of the time is spent on the first layout.
- ~48% of the time is spent in the parser and DOM tree creation

- ~8% is spent on style resolution
- ~5% is spent on collecting the style – this is what we should be testing and what should take most of the time. (The remaining time is spread over many many little functions).

With the test above, let say we have a baseline of 100 ms with the fastest selector. Of that, 5 ms would be spent collecting style. If a second selector is 3 times slower, that would appear as 110 ms in total. The test should report a 300% difference but instead it only shows 10%.

At this point, I responded that whilst I understood what Benjamin was pointing out, my test was only supposed to illustrate that the same page, with all other things being equal, renders largely the same regardless of the selector used. Benjamin took the time to reply with further detail:

> *I completely agree it is useless to optimize selectors upfront, but for completely different reasons:*
> *It is practically impossible to predict the final performance impact of a given selector by just examining the selectors. In the engine, selectors are reordered, split, collected and compiled. To know the final performance of a given selectors, you would have to know in which bucket the selector was collected, how it is compiled, and finally what does the DOM tree looks like.*
> *All of that is very different between the various engines, making the whole process even less predictable.*
> *The second argument I have against web developers optimizing selectors is that they will likely make things worse. The amount of misinformation about selectors is larger than correct cross-browser information. The chance of someone doing the right thing is pretty low.*
> *In practice, people discover performance problems with CSS and start removing rules one by one until the problem go away. I think that is the right way to go about this, it is easy and will lead to correct outcome.*

Cause and effect

At this point I felt vindicated that the CSS selector used was almost entirely irrelevant. However, I did wonder what else we could gleam from the tests.

If the number of DOM elements on the page was halved, as you might expect, the speed to complete any of the tests dropped commensurately. But getting rid of large parts of the DOM isn't always a possibility in the real world. This made me wonder what difference the amount of unused styles in the CSS would have on the results.

What difference does style bloat make?

Another test (`https://benfrain.com/selector-test/2-01.html`): I grabbed a big fat style sheet that had absolutely no relevance to the DOM tree. It was about 3000 lines of CSS. All these irrelevant styles were inserted before a final rule that would select our inner `a.link` node and make it red. I did the same averaging of the results across 5 runs on each browser.

Half those rules were then cut out and the test repeated (`https://benfrain.com/selector-test/2-02.html`) to give a comparison. Here are the results:

Test	Chrome 34	Firefox 29	Opera 19	IE 19	Android 4
Full bloat	64.4	237.6	74.2	436.8	1714.6
Half bloat	51.6	142.8	65.4	358.6	1412.4

Rules diet

This provides some interesting figures. For example, Firefox was 1.7X slower to complete this test than it was with its slowest selector test (test 6). Android 4.3 was 1.2X slower than its slowest selector test (test 6). Internet Explorer was a whopping 2.5X slower than its slowest selector!

You can see that things dropped down considerably for Firefox when half of the styles were removed (approx 1500 lines). The Android device came down to around the speed of its slowest selector at that point too.

Removing unused styles

Does this kind of horror scenario sound familiar to you? Enormous CSS files with all manner of selectors (often with selectors in that don't even work), heaps of ever more specific selectors seven or more levels deep, non-applicable vendor-prefix's, ID selectors all over the place and file sizes of 50–80 KB (sometimes more).

If you are working on a code base that has a big fat CSS file like this, one that no-one is quite sure what all the styles are actually for, my advice would be to look there for your CSS optimisations before the selectors being employed. Hopefully by this point you will be convinced that an ECSS approach might help in this respect.

Then again, that won't necessarily help with the actual performance of your CSS.

Performance inside the brackets

The *final test* (`https://benfrain.com/selector-test/3-01.html`) I ran was to hit the page with a bunch of *expensive* properties and values. Consider this rule:

```
.link {
    background-color: red;
    border-radius: 5px;
    padding: 3px;
    box-shadow: 0 5px 5px #000;
    -webkit-transform: rotate(10deg);
    -moz-transform: rotate(10deg);
    -ms-transform: rotate(10deg);
    transform: rotate(10deg);
    display: block;
}
```

With that rule applied, here are the results:

Test	Chrome 34	Firefox 29	Opera 19	IE 19	Android 4
Expensive Styles	65.2	151.4	65.2	259.2	1923

Here all browsers are at least up with their slowest selector speed (IE was 1.5X slower than its slowest selector test (10) and the Android device was 1.3X slower than the slowest selector test (test 6)) but that's not even the full picture. Try and scroll that page! Repaint on those kind of styles can bring a browser to its knees (or whatever the equivalent of knees is for a browser).

The properties we stick inside the braces are what really affects performance. It stands to reason that scrolling a page that requires endless expensive re-paints and layout changes is going to put a strain on the device. Nice HiDPI screen? It will be even worse as the CPU/GPU strains to get everything re-painted to screen in under 16 ms.

With the expensive styles test, on the 15" Retina MacBook Pro I tested on, the paint time shown in continuous paint mode in Chrome never dropped below 280 ms (and remember, we are aiming for sub–16 ms). To put that in perspective for you, the first selector test page, never went above 2.5 ms. That wasn't a typo. Those properties created a 112X increase in paint time. Holy expensive properties Batman! Indeed Robin. Indeed.

What properties are expensive?

An *expensive* property/value pairing is one we can be pretty confident will make the browser struggle with when it has to repaint the screen (e.g. on scroll).

How can we know what will be an *expensive* style? Thankfully, we can apply common sense to this and get a pretty good idea what is going to tax the browser. Anything that requires a browser to manipulate/calculate before painting to the page will be more costly. For example, box-shadows, border-radius, transparency (as the browser has to calculate what is shown below), transforms and performance killers like CSS filters – if performance is your priority, anything like that is your worst enemy.

 Juriy kangax Zaytsev did `a fantastic blog post also covering CSS performance` (`http://perfectionkills.com/profiling-css-for-fun-and-profit-optimization-notes/`) back in 2012. He was using the various developer tools to measure performance. He did a particularly good job of showing the difference that various properties had on performance. If this kind of thing interests you then that post is well worth your time.

Summary

Some takeaways from these tests:

- Sweating over the selectors used in modern browsers is futile; most selection methods are now so fast it's really not worth spending much time over. Furthermore, there is disparity across browsers of what the slowest selectors are anyway. Look here last to speed up your CSS.
- Excessive unused styles are likely to cost more, performance wise, than any selectors you chose so look to tidy up there second. 3000 lines that are unused or surplus on a page are not even that uncommon. While it's common to bunch all the styles up into a great big single `styles.css`, if different areas of your site/web application can have different (additional) style sheets added (dependency graph style), that may be the better option.

- If your CSS has been added to by a number of different authors over time, look to tools like *UnCSS* (`https://github.com/giakki/uncss`) to automate the removal of styles; doing that process by hand is no fun!
- The battle for high performing CSS will not be won in the selectors used, it will be won with the judicious use of property and values.
- Getting something painted to screen fast is obviously important but so is how a page feels when the user interacts with it. Look for expensive property and value pairs first (Chrome continuous repaint mode is your friend here), they are likely to provide the biggest gains.

Appendix 2

Browser Representatives on CSS Performance

As a companion to `Appendix 1`, *CSS Selector Performance*, the following text deals with what browser representatives have to say about CSS performance.

TL;DR

If you read nothing more of this section, read this next paragraph and take it to heart:

Do not memorize rules in relation to CSS performance without checking your own *data*. They are largely useless, transient and too subjective. Instead become acquainted with tools and use them to reveal relevant data for your own scenario. This is basically the mantra the Chrome Developer relations folks have been promoting for years, I believe it was Paul Lewis (more of which below) that coined the term, *Tools, not rules* in relation to troubleshooting web performance.

Nowadays I get that sentiment. Really get it.

Browser representatives on CSS performance

While I generally never worry CSS selectors when authoring a style sheet (typically I just put a class on anything I want to style and select it directly) every so often I see comments from people way smarter than me that relate specifically to a certain selector. Here's a quote from *Paul Irish* (`https://www.paulirish.com/`) in relation to a *post on A List Apart from Heydon Pickering* (`http://alistapart.com/article/quantity-queries-for-css`) which used a specific type of selector:

> *These selectors are among the slowest possible. ~500 slower than something wild like div.box:not(:empty):last-of-type .title". Test page http://jsbin.com/gozula/1/quiet That said, selector speed is rarely a concern, but if this selector ends up in a dynamic webapp where DOM changes are very common, it could have a large effect. So, good for many use cases but keep in mind it might become a perf bottleneck as the app matures. Something to profile at that point. Cheers*

What are we to take from that? Do we try and hold that kind of selector in some *do not use in case of emergency* vault in our heads?

To try and get some *real* answers, I asked the smart folks who actually work on browsers what they think we should concern ourselves with in regards to CSS performance.

In the front-end world we are lucky that the Chrome Developer relations team are so accessible. However, I like balance. In addition, I reached out to people at Microsoft and Firefox and included some great input from WebKit too.

Should we worry about CSS selectors?

The question was essentially, *Should authors concern themselves with the selectors used in relation to CSS performance?*

Let's start at the beginning, where things like the CSSOM and DOM actually get constructed. *Paul Lewis* (`http://aerotwist.com/`), Developer Advocate for Chrome Developer Relations explains, *Style calculations are affected by two things: selector matching and the size of the invalidation. When you first load a page all the styles need to be calculated for all the elements, and that's a function of tree size and the number of selectors.*

For more detail, Lewis quotes *Rune Lillesveen* (https://docs.google.com/document/d/1vE W86DaeVs4uQzNFI5R-_xS9TcS1Cs_EUsHRSgCHGu8/edit#) on the Opera team (who does a lot of work on Blink's style code):

> *At the time of writing, roughly 50% of the time used to calculate the computed style for an element is used to match selectors, and the other half of the time is used for constructing the RenderStyle (computed style representation) from the matched rules.*

OK, that went a bit *science* for me so does that mean we need to worry about selectors or not?

Lewis again, *Selector matching can affect performance, but in my experience the tree size tends to be the most significant factor.*

It stands to reason that if you have an enormous DOM tree, and a whole raft of irrelevant styles, things are going to start chugging. My own *bloat test* (https://benfrain.com/selec tor-test/2-01.html) backs this up. Consider this another way. If I give you two piles of 1000 cards, each with different names on except for 5 matching ones, it stands to reason it will take longer to pair those matching names than if there were only 100, or 10 cards. Same principal for the browser.

I think we can all agree that style bloat is a bigger concern than the CSS selector used. Maybe that's one rule we can bank on?

> *For most websites I would posit that selector performance is not the best area to spend your time trying to find performance optimizations. I would highly recommend to focus on what is inside the braces than the selectors outside of them*
> *-Greg Whitworth, Program Manager at Microsoft*

What about JavaScript

However, Whitworth also notes that extra diligence is required when dealing with JavaScript and dynamism in the DOM structure, *If you are using JavaScript to add or replace classes on events over and over again you should think about how that will affect the overall web pipeline and the DOM structure of the box you're touching.*

This ties in with the earlier comment from *Paul Irish* (https://www.paulirish.com/). Rapid invalidation of areas of the DOM thanks to class changes can occasionally show up complex selectors. So, maybe we should be worried about selectors?

> *There are exceptions to every rule and there are selectors that are more performant than others but we normally only see these in cases where there are massive DOM trees in tandem with JavaScript anti-patterns that causes DOM thrashing and additional layout or painting to take place*
> *-Whitworth*

For more simplistic JavaScript changes, Lewis offers this advice, *The solution is normally to target elements as closely as possible, though increasingly Blink is smart about which elements will truly be affected by a change to a parent element.* So, practically speaking, if you need to affect a change in a DOM element, add a class directly above it in the DOM tree if possible, rather than up on the body or html node.

Dealing with CSS performance

At this point I'm happily re-concluding the conclusion arrived at in `Appendix 1`, *CSS Selector Performance* – that CSS selectors are rarely a problem with static pages. Plus, attempting to second guess which selector will perform well is probably futile.

However, for large DOMs and dynamic DOMs (e.g. not the odd class toggle, we are talking lots of JavaScript manipulation) it may not be beyond the realms of possibility that CSS selectors could be causing an issue. *I can't speak for all of Mozilla, but I think when you're dealing with performance, you want to focus on what's slow. Sometimes that will be selectors; usually it will be other things,* says *L. David Baron* (`http://dbaron.org/`), of *Mozilla* (`https://www.mozilla.org/en-US/`) and a member of the W3C's CSS working group. *I've definitely seen pages where selector performance matters, and I've definitely seen lots of pages where it doesn't.*

So what should we do? What's the most pragmatic approach?

> *You should use profiling tools to determine where your performance problems are, and then work on solving those problems*
> *-Baron*

Everyone I spoke to echoed these sentiments.

Summary

If you've developed on the Web for any non-trivial period of time you will know that the answer to most web related questions is *it depends*. I hate that there are no simple, cast-iron rules in relation to CSS performance that can be banked upon in every situation. I'd genuinely love to write those rules out here in a nice little paragraph and believe they would be universally true. But I can't because there simply aren't any universal *cast-iron* truths in relation to performance. There can't ever be any because there are simply too many variables. Engines update, layout methods become optimised, every DOM tree is different, all CSS files are different. On and on ad infinitum. You get the picture.

I'm afraid the best I can offer is to not sweat things like CSS selectors or layout methods in advance. It's unlikely they will be your problem (but, you know, they just might). Instead, concentrate on making *the thing*. Then, when *the thing* is made, test *the thing*. If it's slow or broke, find the problem and fix *the thing*.

Additional Information

- Greg Whitworth recommends *A 2012 Build talk* (`http://blogs.msdn.com/b/ie/a rchive/2012/11/20/build-2012-50-performance-tricks-to-make-your-html 5-applications-and-sites-faster.aspx`)
- *CSS Triggers* (`https://csstriggers.com/`) by Paul Lewis indicates what changes in CSS will trigger Layout, Paint and Composite operations in the Blink engine (Chrome/Opera)

Index

www.ingramcontent.com/pod-product-compliance
Lightning Source LLC
Chambersburg PA
CBHW060151060326
40690CB00018B/4070